# Cardozo

# Cardozo

## A Study in Reputation

Richard A. Posner

The University of Chicago Press

*Chicago and London*

RICHARD A. POSNER is a judge on the Seventh
Circuit, U.S. Court of Appeals. He has taught at
Stanford University Law School and the
University of Chicago Law School and is the
author of numerous books, including
*Antitrust Law: An Economic Perspective;*
*Law and Literature: A Misunderstood Relation;*
and *The Problems of Jurisprudence.*
He lives in Chicago.

The University of Chicago Press, Chicago 60637
The University of Chicago Press, Ltd., London

© 1990 by The University of Chicago
All rights reserved. Published 1990
Printed in the United States of America

99 98 97 96 95 94 93 92 91 90    5 4 3 2 1

Library of Congress Cataloging-in-Publication Data

Posner, Richard A.
    Cardozo : a study in reputation / Richard A. Posner.
        p.    cm.
    Includes index.
    ISBN 0-226-67555-6
        1. Cardozo, Benjamin N. (Benjamin Nathan), 1870–1938.    2. Judges—
United States—Biography.    I. Title.
    KF8745.C3P64    1990
    347.73′14—dc20                                                90-35479
    [347.30714]                                                   CIP

# Contents

BENJAMIN NATHAN CARDOZO.
Detail of a print by Franklin R. Wood.
Reproduced by permission of the
Harvard Law Art Collection.

# Introduction

THIS BOOK IS THE revised and expanded text of the Cooley
Lectures that I had the honor to give at the University of
Michigan Law School on November 13–15, 1989. In casting
about for a suitable topic for the lectures, I was mindful not only
of the Michigan Law School's eminence both in jurisprudence and
in law and literature but also of my own recent interest in both
fields.[1] I wanted a topic that would combine the two areas, relate
to my current vocation as an appellate judge, and relate as well
to my continuing interest in the economic analysis of law. I found
that topic in the career of Benjamin Cardozo. The most "literary"
of our judges in a sense to be explained, Cardozo was also a
distinguished contributor to jurisprudence—the philosophy of
law—advocating a form of legal pragmatism that resembles the
pragmatism advocated in my book on jurisprudence (note 1).
And not only are many of his judicial opinions interesting from
an economic standpoint (almost all judicial opinions are potentially interesting from that standpoint); economic analysis of
reputation is helpful in unraveling the mystery of Cardozo's reputation. Mystery there is. Although the legal establishment can-
onized Cardozo during his lifetime and he is still widely
considered not merely one of the greatest judges of all time but
a judicial saint, there is a considerable, perhaps an increasing,
undercurrent of dubiety. Today many legal thinkers believe that

1. See my books *Law and Literature: A Misunderstood Relation* (1988); *The Problems of Jurisprudence* (1990).

Cardozo has been greatly overrated—that his liberalism is a fake, his judicial philosophy a bunch of platitudes, his famous writing style obese and archaic. More are unsure how he should be ranked, and indeed whether any judge can be evaluated on an objective scale of merit.

There are essays galore that attempt to evaluate the work of individual judges, and there are some although not many judicial biographies. But so far as I am aware, there are no monograph-length studies, evaluative rather than biographical, social scientific as well as legal doctrinal, critical not pious, of individual judges; certainly there is none of Benjamin Cardozo. Not all gaps are worth filling. But this one—or rather two: a gap in genres of judicial study and the specific neglect of an enormously prominent judge—is. When one considers that the appellate judge is the central figure in Anglo-American jurisprudence, the dearth of evaluative writing on individual judges that is at once systematic, nonpolitical, and nonpolemical is remarkable. The full-length critical (not biographical) judicial study, employing tools of social science as well as of legal doctrine, is a nonexistent genre, which this book aspires to create. The endeavor requires that I refine the tools of judicial evaluation and the very concept of "reputation" as well as attend closely to the texture of Cardozo's writing and thought, much as one would do in a critical study of the work of a poet or a philosopher.

The first chapter reviews the essential biographical facts as an aid to assessing Cardozo's character, which I argue equipped him well for a distinguished career as an appellate judge. It also reviews the previous assessments of Cardozo and notes the surprisingly ambivalent tone of many of those assessments: his reputation among academics is by no means as assured as one might have expected. Chapter 2 discusses Cardozo's judicial philosophy, primarily as expounded in his best-known book, *The Nature of the Judicial Process*. I argue that Cardozo was an authentic legal pragmatist in the tradition of Oliver Wendell Holmes and, especially,

John Dewey. Indeed, I regard Cardozo as the canonical expositor, and *The Nature of the Judicial Process* as the canonical exposition, of that judicial faith. Chapter 3 begins the process of assessing Cardozo's judicial technique, through a close examination of several opinions (principally *Palsgraf* and *Hynes*) considered in conjunction with the lawyers' briefs and the trial records. I emphasize his considerable narrative skills and his adroit selection of facts as some—not all—of the keys to his judicial distinction. But I also stress both the weak sense of fact, characteristic of much legal pragmatism, that mars many of his opinions, and the normative ambiguity of rhetorical power in judicial opinions as in other texts.

With chapter 4, I turn briefly away from Cardozo to examine the issue of reputation both generally and with respect to judges. What is "reputation"? Is it the summation of a person's worth, and if so, is it proportional to that worth? Or is it the exploitation of one person's doings or sayings for the exploiter's own purposes? (I think it is a mixture of both things.) Can it be measured? In particular, can judicial reputations be measured? Even if reputation can be measured, can it be equated to quality? To influence? If not, how can these attributes be distinguished empirically?

Against this background, chapter 5 offers a number of quantitative assessments of Cardozo's reputation. For example, it compares the number of times his judicial opinions are cited by other judges, discussed by legal scholars, and reprinted in casebooks with the number of times opinions of other judges of the New York Court of Appeals during Cardozo's tenure are cited, discussed, and reprinted. These comparisons provide objective (though not conclusive) evidence that Cardozo was indeed an outstanding judge and in so doing may help to dispel the ambivalence noted in the first chapter. Chapters 4 and 5 are the methodologically most novel chapters of the book and will, I hope, interest scholars in other fields as well as in law.

Chapter 6 undertakes a closer examination of Cardozo's opinions (emphasizing those he wrote for the New York Court of Appeals), with a view toward making an independent evaluation of the nature and quality of his judicial performance, as well as toward providing additional clues to the causes of his reputation. I emphasize the moralistic tone of his opinions and relate it to his dominant judicial project—a highly worthy one when properly understood, and one by no means completed—of bringing the law into closer conformity with lay intuitions of fair dealing. Chapter 7 ties together the strands of the analysis. It first summarizes the factors that appear to be responsible for Cardozo's great reputation, including his skills (personal as well as intellectual) and tactics, the importance in his day of the New York Court of Appeals as a commercial court, the boost that Cardozo's reputation received from his appointment to the United States Supreme Court, and intrinsic characteristics of the "market" in reputations. I emphasize Cardozo's rhetorical distinction and argue—what is likely to prove, along with the proposition that reputation can fruitfully be studied quantitatively, my most controversial claim—that rhetorical power may be a more important attribute of judicial excellence than analytical power. (The controversiality of this point is also, I argue, a clue to the ambivalence of Cardozo's reputation among academic lawyers.) I then offer my evaluation of Cardozo's place in history, with particular attention to his strengths and weaknesses vis-à-vis those of several other famous judges, such as Oliver Wendell Holmes and Learned Hand.

In a brief epilogue, I discuss a number of possible avenues for further research that are suggested by this study. I both suggest ways in which the genre of the critical judicial study can be refined and developed and urge research into two neglected subjects in judicial administration: the best system for assigning judicial opinions and the desirability of signed opinions versus per curiam (anonymous) ones.

As should be evident from even so brief a synopsis, this is not a book for lawyers only. The American judiciary is a fascinating and important social institution, and prominent judges like Cardozo are figures in the history and practice of rhetoric and philosophy as well as of law. The tools of legal reasoning are not adequate to the evaluation of a Cardozo; it is a task for interdisciplinary study. To make the book intelligible to the nonlawyer, I have had to explain certain terms that are obvious to lawyers— to whom I apologize in advance for any tedium these explanations may engender.

I have fewer apologies than I have acknowledgments. First of all I thank Dean Bollinger and the Michigan faculty for honoring me with an invitation to deliver the Cooley Lectures, thereby stimulating my search for a suitable topic that has led to this book; for their hospitality during my visit to Ann Arbor to deliver the lectures; and for their many helpful suggestions. I thank Steven Hetcher, Erick Kaardal, Catherine O'Neill, Adam Pritchard, and Barbara Smith for their excellent research assistance, and Michael Aronson, Douglas Baird, Dennis Black, Philip Elman, Robert Ferguson, William Landes, John Langbein, Lawrence Lessig, Sanford Levinson, Charlene Posner, Eric Posner, Max Posner, Brian Simpson, Cass Sunstein, Richard Weisberg, G. Edward White, and participants in a Work in Progress Luncheon at the University of Chicago Law School on January 11, 1990, for many helpful comments on a previous draft. I owe special debts to Anthony Grech, Curator of the Association of the Bar of the City of New York, and Judith Wright, Director of the D'Angelo Law Library of the University of Chicago Law School, for assistance in obtaining access to the briefs and records in cases decided by the New York Court of Appeals during Cardozo's tenure there; to Wright for additional bibliographical assistance as well; to Dennis Hutchinson for many very stimulating comments and suggestions on the draft and conversations about the subject matter; and to Frank Easterbrook for meticulous and helpful comments on the draft. Finally, I owe a very special debt to

Andrew Kaufman, for sharing with me portions of his forthcoming biography of Cardozo, for conversation and correspondence on Cardozo's life and work, and for exceptionally generous and invariably helpful comments on not one but two previous drafts.

With all the help I have had, the reader can rest assured that the errors that remain are indeed my own.

# I

## The Life, the Person,
## the Reputation

THE ESSENTIAL FACTS OF Cardozo's life can be stated briefly.[1]
Benjamin Nathan Cardozo was born in 1870 in New York
City to a distinguished Sephardic Jewish family that had come
to this country in the eighteenth century.[2] He and his twin sister
were the youngest of six children (a seventh died in infancy).
Cardozo's father, Albert, was a justice of the Supreme Court of
New York; that is, he was a judge of the state trial court of
general jurisdiction. Shortly after Benjamin's birth, he had to

1. The only full-length biography of Cardozo is an uncritical, undocumented
work by a friend, written shortly after Cardozo's death: George S. Hellman, *Benjamin N. Cardozo: American Judge* (1940). Of the same vintage but more analytical
is Beryl Harold Levy, *Cardozo and Frontiers of Legal Thinking, with Selected Opinions*
(1938). For brief biographical treatments, see Andrew L. Kaufman, "Benjamin
Cardozo," in *The Justices of the United States Supreme Court 1789–1969: Their Lives
and Major Opinions*, vol. 3, p. 2287 (Leon Friedman and Fred L. Israel eds. 1969);
G. Edward White, *The American Judicial Tradition: Profiles of Leading American Judges*
254–260 (expanded ed. 1988). Paul Bricker, "Justice Benjamin N. Cardozo: A
Fresh Look at a Great Judge," 11 *Ohio Northern University Law Review* 1, 24–29
(1984), contains some interesting biographical information. Hellman's book contains a number of personal recollections of Cardozo; for others, see "A Personal
View of Justice Benjamin N. Cardozo: Recollections of Four Cardozo Law Clerks,"
1 *Cardozo Law Review* 5 (1979); Milton Handler and Michael Ruby, "Justice Cardozo, One-Ninth of the Supreme Court," 10 *Cardozo Law Review* 235 (1988); Arthur L. Corbin, "The Judicial Process Revisited: Introduction," 71 *Yale Law
Journal* 195 (1961). Professor Kaufman has been working for many years on the
first full-length critical biography of Cardozo and has been kind enough to share
with me a chapter in which he discusses Cardozo's personal life.

2. For a popular history of New York's Sephardic community, see Stephen Birmingham, *The Grandees: America's Sephardic Elite* (1971). Chapter 18 is about the
Cardozos.

resign his judgeship to avoid being impeached for having done judicial favors for the Tweed Ring. He was not disbarred, however, and practiced law successfully after his resignation.

Cardozo's mother died when he was nine, followed six years later by his father. Cardozo was raised mainly by his eldest sister, Ellen ("Nell"). Apparently Albert Cardozo left enough money to enable his family to live comfortably, although not opulently, in the family home on Madison Avenue. Ben, as his family and a few close friends called him, was tutored at home (by Horatio Alger, no less) and entered Columbia College at the age of fifteen. His college studies were concentrated in the humanities, with special emphasis on philosophy. Graduating at or near the top of his class at the age of nineteen, he then entered Columbia Law School but, as was common in those days, left after two years without bothering to take a degree. Probably he was eager to begin practice in order to earn a living, since at the time his elder brother was the only breadwinner in the family.

Cardozo joined his father's old firm. The distinction of Cardozo's family, which survived the blot that Albert had placed on the family escutcheon, and Cardozo's own personal style appear to have protected Cardozo from overt anti-Semitism until he encountered the egregious McReynolds on the Supreme Court.[3] Yet Cardozo's law practice appears to have been confined to the Jewish business and legal community. He was a highly successful trial lawyer, specializing in the later years of his practice in appellate litigation; during this period he wrote a lucid although not exciting treatise for practitioners on the jurisdiction of the New York Court of Appeals.[4] His reputation at the bar was excellent, and in 1913, after more than two decades of practice, he was

3. It is true that Cardozo may have been passed over for the Supreme Court several times because of his Judaism—more particularly because there was already one Jew (Brandeis) on the Court. But should this be called anti-Semitism? Ethnic balance, including the avoidance of ethnic imbalance, has long been a consideration in appointments to the Supreme Court, as in political appointment generally.

4. *The Jurisdiction of the Court of Appeals of the State of New York* (2d ed. 1909).

slated to run on the Democratic ticket for justice of the Supreme Court of New York. Excellence was not his only credential. The slatemakers wanted a Jew on the ticket. In addition, although Cardozo was never involved in partisan politics, he was a Democrat accurately perceived to be a liberal (in the progressive, later the New Deal, sense), and his slating may have reflected in part a desire to liberalize the New York courts, which had acquired a reputation for being hostile to labor interests.[5] Cardozo was elected. After only a month on the state supreme court, he was breveted to the New York Court of Appeals (New York's highest court) to help with that court's heavy workload.[6] There he remained. Despite his comparative youth and his lack of judicial experience, he was an immediate hit both with his colleagues and with the bar, and in 1917 he was elected to the court of appeals with the endorsement of both major political parties.

In part reflecting New York's commercial preeminence, in part the quality of its personnel, the New York Court of Appeals was the nation's most distinguished common law tribunal, and Cardozo, who from the outset was the court's brightest star, soon became widely touted as the nation's leading common law judge. He was also one of the founders of the American Law Institute and was active in its affairs, as well as being a distinguished lecturer on jurisprudence; these extrajudicial activities further enhanced his reputation. In 1927 he was elected chief judge of the court of appeals, again with bipartisan support. He served in that post until appointed in 1932 by President Hoover to succeed Holmes on the United States Supreme Court. The appointment to the Supreme Court was a fluke.[7] Cardozo was a New Yorker,

5. Francis Bergan, *The History of the New York Court of Appeals, 1847–1932* 245–247 (1985); William C. Cunningham, "Cardozo's Theory of Judicial Decision: Opinions and Off-the-Bench Writings 1914–1932," at pp. 2-2 and 2-3 (Columbia D. Sci. L. diss. 1972).

6. The court of appeals was authorized to appoint up to four supreme court justices as temporary court of appeals judges.

7. The story is well told in Andrew L. Kaufman, "Cardozo's Appointment to

a Jew, and a Democrat; the Court already had one Jew and two New Yorkers, and Hoover, of course, was a Republican. And while Cardozo may or may not have wanted the job—he seems to have had genuinely mixed feelings about it, yet accepted Hoover's offer on the spot—it appears that he didn't raise a finger to get it.[8] Although not a sufficient condition of the appointment, it was a necessary condition that Cardozo was a famous and universally respected jurist. Enormously well regarded by lawyers and judges (notably including Justice Stone, a friend of Hoover's) because of his personal as well as his professional qualities, Cardozo was enthusiastically supported for the appointment by the organized bar, the academy, and the media. But apparently what put him over the top was a dearth of politically acceptable alternatives, and perhaps a felt need by Hoover— facing a tough reelection campaign in a few months—to make a nonpolitical appointment to the Supreme Court.

Cardozo came from a family of short-lived and rather sickly individuals. The average age at death of Cardozo, his parents, and his siblings, excluding the one who died in infancy, was fifty-three; only Ben (sixty-eight) and Nell (seventy) reached sixty. A contributing factor may have been inbreeding within the small Sephardic community; "both sets of [Cardozo's] grandparents had been marriages of cousins, as had at least two sets of . . . great-grandparents."[9] Cardozo was already suffering from coronary artery disease when he joined the Supreme Court, but despite his poor health he took on more than his share of the Court's work. He became identified with the Court's liberals, Brandeis and Stone, although he was close personally and professionally only

---

the Supreme Court," 1 *Cardozo Law Review* 23 (1979), and in Ira H. Carmen, "The President, Politics and the Power of Appointment: Hoover's Nomination of Mr. Justice Cardozo," 55 *Virginia Law Review* 616 (1969). Of course, any Supreme Court appointment is, ex ante, a low-probability event.

8. On Cardozo's refusal to campaign for appointment to the Supreme Court, see id. at 619–620, 653; Kaufman, note 7 above, at 48–50.

9. Birmingham, note 2 above, at 300.

to the latter. Felled by a heart attack in December, 1937, followed by a stroke in January, 1938, a few months short of his sixth anniversary on the Court, Cardozo did not recover sufficiently to return to duty. He died in the summer of 1938.

Cardozo never married, and this, his close relationship with his eldest sister, and the disgrace of his father are the biographical facts around which efforts at his psychobiography pivot.[10] There are rumors that Cardozo's correspondence with Nell, with whom he lived until her death in 1929, and which Cardozo largely destroyed, depicts an unusually close relationship,[11] although there is no reason to think that the relationship was sexual. Nell was eleven years older than he and had brought him up after their mother died. Cardozo had a strong sense of family, and Nell was by all accounts a woman of wit and intelligence. Their relationship was a good deal closer than that of the average sister and brother—perhaps more like that of a mother and a son who finds it difficult to form mature relationships with other women.

The disgrace of Cardozo's father is a fact; given Cardozo's sensitivity and pride in family, it must have stung, but with what effect on his career it is impossible to say. Cardozo's opinions and extrajudicial writings display a strong streak of moralism, but this is easily accounted for without supposing that he was trying to compensate for his father's moral derelictions.

That Cardozo never married is also a fact. Part of the explanation may lie in a suggestion by one of his former law clerks, Alan M. Stroock. After noting the social aloofness of New York's

10. Psychobiography is a controversial genre, and efforts at judicial psychobiography, illustrated by H. N. Hirsch, *The Enigma of Felix Frankfurter* (1981), and by Robert A. Burt, *Two Jewish Justices: Outcasts in the Promised Land* (1988), have not been well received. See, for example, Eben Moglen's review of Burt's book, 89 *Columbia Law Review* 959 (1989); also references in id. at 969 n. 18. The most plausible effort at judicial psychobiography that I have found is the psychological profile of three unnamed trial judges in Harold Dwight Lasswell, *Power and Personality* 65–88 (1948). Whether it is accurate or not is a separate question impossible to answer because the judges' identities are not revealed.

11. White, note 1 above, at 497 n. 14.

small Sephardic community, Stroock remarks: "Not only did the Justice never marry; only one of his [three] sisters married, presumably because no suitable mates could be found."[12] Cardozo was unlikely to marry outside New York's Sephardic community, and this greatly restricted the field of selection. Add to this the fact that Cardozo was shy and fastidious, hard-working and ambitious, and physically frail, and it becomes easier to understand why he never married, without delving into psychiatric speculation.

Scholars of psychiatric bent might, however, want to explore the possible significance of the fact that Cardozo's mother died when he was a child and his father when Cardozo was an adolescent, and that Cardozo's twin was a girl. "Patients growing up in families where one or both of the parents died appear more compromised in their interpersonal relationships . . . These patients are more likely to have impairments in achieving stable, mature adult attachments."[13] Cardozo's relationship with Nell, and his (quite possibly related) failure to marry, is consistent with this observation. As for having a twin of the opposite sex, it has been suggested that this can result in the "feminizing" of the male twin and the "masculinizing" of the female.[14] This suggestion might, if true, help explain Cardozo's failure to marry. Yet his twin was his only sibling to marry! I shall not pursue these questions further; the details of Cardozo's psychology, so far as they are known, seem tenuously, if at all, related to his professional work, which is my interest.

All accounts agree on Cardozo's salient traits as a person. He was extremely intelligent, very hardworking, bookish, and exceedingly polite. The intelligence and hard work are necessary

12. "A Personal View of Justice Benjamin N. Cardozo: Recollections of Four Cardozo Law Clerks," note 1 above, at 20. Cardozo's only brother also never married.

13. Paul V. Ragan and Thomas H. McGlashan, "Childhood Parental Death and Adult Psychopathology," 143 *American Journal of Psychiatry* 153, 156 (1986).

14. Amram Scheinfeld, *Twins and Supertwins* 191–192 (1967).

conditions of the professional eminence that Cardozo attained, the bookishness is important in explaining the literary flair evident in his opinions, the politeness helps explain his popularity with bench and bar and his influence with his colleagues on the New York Court of Appeals. He wrote all his judicial opinions (as well as all his books and essays) himself. He did not have law clerks in the modern sense until he joined the Supreme Court, and he made relatively little use even of his Supreme Court clerks—much less than Brandeis, let alone than a modern judge—but more than Holmes had done. Cardozo would discuss the cases with his clerk before conference (Supreme Court justices had only one clerk in those days, not four, as most of them have today) and, by their account anyway, was receptive to the clerk's suggestions. But he delegated no opinion writing to the clerk and did most of his own research. A sign of his politeness is that he rarely adopted an adversarial stance toward lawyers or lower-court judges, either in person or in his opinions; the only exception I am aware of is his treatment of the lower-court judges in the *Hynes* case, discussed in chapter 3. Of course, he lived in an era when lawyers and judges—perhaps people in general—were more civil than they are today.

My description so far of Cardozo would fit any number of other distinguished judges. All I have said really is that Cardozo was intelligent, well read, hardworking, decorous, courteous, and independent of his law clerks. The difference between Cardozo and other eminent American judges is that he is the only "saint" among them.[15] The appellation is misleading if we associate saintliness with intense religious conviction, heroism, unusual altruism, or self-denial. Cardozo appears to have had no religious

15. "By the unanimous testimony of his contemporaries, Cardozo was a saint." Grant Gilmore, *The Ages of American Law* 75 (1977) (footnote omitted—and from now on I omit footnotes in quoted material without remarking the fact). Richard H. Weisberg, "Law, Literature and Cardozo's Judicial Poetics," 1 *Cardozo Law Review* 283, 284, 287 (1979), speaks in like vein of Cardozo's "sainthood" and "almost angelic presence."

beliefs, was never called on to display and never did display heroic qualities, was not conspicuously altruistic outside his own family, was not without ambition and antipathies, and contrary to legend was not given to self-denial beyond that implicit in his celibate state. No saint has ever been a successful trial lawyer. Cardozo was not a high liver, but this may have been due to his physical frailty; he lived quite comfortably and disapproved of Brandeis's ostentatious austerity.[16] The people who call Cardozo a saint know little about saints and have succumbed to the American habit of sanctifying law.

The impression of "saintliness" in the loose sense derives from the well-attested gentleness, modesty, tact, considerateness, mildness, circumspection, judiciousness, and moderation of the Cardozo persona. It went beyond politeness and noncombativeness. He can't have been quite the angel the idolaters assert but he plainly was a nice man, and if this equates to sainthood it is a testament to the character or lack thereof of great judges. It is not that he lacked forthrightness in stating and arguing for his views; quite the contrary. Yet despite this he seems never to have given serious offense. One has to *be* a judge to know how difficult an achievement that was, especially for a judge as prominent and ambitious as Cardozo, one who would naturally attract the envy and resentment of less gifted colleagues.

A number of strands in Cardozo's personality explain this phenomenon. First, he had a gentle, diffident manner; he was not in the least overbearing. Second, he had uncommonly good manners. Third, he was effusive in his praise of others; yet unlike Frankfurter he was not really a flatterer, because his effusions encompassed people to whom he could not look for advancement, such as his law clerks.[17] Fourth, he was considerate of other peo-

---

16. I rely on Stroock again. "A Personal View of Justice Benjamin N. Cardozo: Recollections of Four Cardozo Law Clerks," note 1 above, at 21–22.

17. "He treated his law clerks with the most flattering solicitude and praised

ple's feelings—and again, regardless of any possible advantage to himself.[18] Fifth, he was a modest, although not a falsely modest, person. He did not lack self-esteem or fail to realize that he was an outstanding judge, but he was aware that even an outstanding person is prone to error and has much to learn from others, including the young. Sixth—and perhaps subtending many of the previous points—Cardozo was an essentially moderate person. He held no extreme views, whether political or methodological, and had no violent convictions; his was not a partisan personality (in contrast to a Frankfurter, a Jackson, or a Black). He was a cautious liberal, a moderate progressive, holding slightly advanced views for his day but not holding them with such passion as might have made him angry with people who disagreed. Not caring passionately about getting one's own way is, however, a very effective way of getting one's own way in a collegial setting such as that of an appellate court. It also facilitates judicial leadership. The judge who is not passionate in his convictions will find it easier to modify his views for the sake of forging a majority position. This is not intellectual dishonesty. It simply is easier to see the strength of another person's point of view if you are not passionately committed on a question. But a judge without convictions will be a leaf in the wind.

Cardozo was not a saint, and there was probably an element of calculation in his demeanor. But he was fundamentally a good and gentle soul, who while eager to shine was remarkably unaggressive by the standards of public men. His character was an asset to his career and to his reputation—to which I now turn.

Cardozo is generally placed in the highest rank of American judges,[19] along with Holmes, John Marshall, Brandeis, and

---

them for whatever they did." "A Personal View of Justice Benjamin N. Cardozo: Recollections of Four Cardozo Law Clerks," note 1 above, at 21 (Stroock). Cardozo enjoyed being praised, too; this is typical of effusive praisers.

18. Handler gives a nice example. Handler and Ruby, note 1 above, at 244.

19. See, for example, Paul A. Freund, "Foreword: Homage to Mr. Justice Car-

Learned Hand. The central question that this book addresses is whether he deserves this high rank. What makes it an interesting question is that there are and long have been doubters. His first and still most prominent detractor was Jerome Frank, himself a prominent judge and legal theorist, who ridiculed Cardozo's style in an article published anonymously shortly after Cardozo's death.[20] Frank calls Cardozo one of our greatest judges and purports to reserve his criticisms for Cardozo's writing style. But the praise is sarcastic and condescending. "Cardozo attained eminence as a thinker not because but in spite of his style. To force himself to think in a foreign tongue [eighteenth-century English, according to Frank] must have cost him much effort. That with such a handicap he thought clearly is a tribute to his genius" (p. 637). "He was a nice analyst with a zest, not always exercised, for following up all the implications of his ideas. But the clarity was in his thinking. His was not a lucid style" (p. 638). Frank compares Cardozo to Black, Douglas, and Jackson, all of whom in Frank's opinion "write in their native tongue. Of Cardozo one might say this: He admitted that, at times, he wrote with his tongue in cheek. And, frequently, it was not even his native tongue" (p. 641). "His writings have grace. But it is an alien grace" (p. 630).

This view of Cardozo's style is widely shared[21] and plainly goes

---

dozo," 1 *Cardozo Law Review* 1 (1979); Bernard Schwartz, "The Judicial Ten: America's Greatest Judges," 1979 *Southern Illinois University Law Journal* 405, 424–428; Bricker, note 1 above; Bernard Weissman, "Cardozo: 'All-Time Greatest' American Judge," 19 *Cumberland Law Review* 1 (1988); Edgar Bodenheimer, "Cardozo's Views on Law and Adjudication Revisited," 22 *University of California Davis Law Review* 1095–1096 (1989); Weisberg, note 15 above.

20. Anon Y. Mous, "The Speech of Judges: A Dissenting Opinion," 29 *Virginia Law Review* 625 (1943). Subsequent page references to this article are in the text.

21. At the opposite extreme from Frank is Richard H. Weisberg, professor at the Benjamin N. Cardozo School of Law (natch), who regards Cardozo's style as exemplary of good legal writing. Weisberg, note 15 above; Weisberg, *When Lawyers Write* 10–11, 45, 257 (1987).

to substance as well as form. Whether it is just I postpone to later chapters. But the style of Frank's attack, along with his decision to publish it anonymously, suggests that Frank was jealous of Cardozo's reputation. If Frank hadn't himself been Jewish, the references to Cardozo's "alien grace" compared to the nativist grace of the three Anglo-Saxon Protestant judges with whom Frank compares Cardozo might invite an accusation of anti-Semitism. Of course, there are anti-Semitic Jews; maybe Frank was one; he seems at the least to have been ambivalent about Judaism.[22]

Much of the criticism of Cardozo belongs to an oral tradition. I recall when I was a first-year student at Harvard Law School in 1959 my torts professor criticizing Cardozo for using metaphors and aphorisms that in the professor's view muddied the law. *His* professor, Warren Seavey, author of a warm encomium to Cardozo,[23] used to deride Cardozo's aphoristic style and to warn the students that "anyone who states on the exam 'danger invites rescue'[24] invites an F." And when I told my academic colleagues at the University of Chicago Law School that I was going to be lecturing on Cardozo, I encountered a polarity of views—some

22. Sanford Levinson, "Writing about Realism" (Review of Robert Jerome Glennon, *The Iconoclast as Reformer: Jerome Frank's Impact on American Law* [1985]), 1985 *American Bar Foundation Research Journal* 899, 902–903.

23. Warren A. Seavey, "Mr. Justice Cardozo and the Law of Torts," 52 *Harvard Law Review* 372 (1939). This is one of the *Essays Dedicated to Mr. Justice Cardozo* (1939) (originally published in volume 39 of the *Columbia Law Review*, volume 52 of the *Harvard Law Review*, and volume 48 of the *Yale Law Journal*). Another, by Arthur Corbin, is cited in note 30 below. Incidentally, the publication the year after Cardozo's death of a Cardozo commemorative issue by the nation's three leading law reviews, plus the later publication of the "Benjamin Nathan Cardozo Commemorative Issue" that in 1979, forty years after Cardozo's death, inaugurated the law review of the newly founded Benjamin N. Cardozo Law School of Yeshiva University, are signs of the magnitude of Cardozo's professional reputation.

24. One of Cardozo's famous aphorisms, from *Wagner v. International Ry.*, which I discuss in chapter 6. Seavey discusses *Wagner* approvingly in his article, note 23 above, at 380–381. Maybe he just thought that "danger invites rescue" mesmerized students.

of these professors thinking he was a great judge, others that he was terrible ("Carbozo"). Of course, academics tend to embrace polar views, especially in conversation.

Many of the published critiques are, like Frank's, ambivalent. Grant Gilmore, in his book *The Ages of American Law* (1977), terms Cardozo "mysterious . . . almost mystical," and remarks that he "apparently felt that his mission was to redeem his father's sins" and "decided at an early age to renounce the pleasures and temptations of the world in favor of a life of intellectual meditation" (p. 74). Although "a truly innovative judge of a type which had long since gone out of fashion" (p. 75), Cardozo

> was accustomed to hide his light under a bushel. The more innovative the decision to which he had persuaded his brethren on the court, the more his opinion strained to prove that no novelty—not the slightest departure from prior law—was involved. Since Cardozo was one of the best case lawyers who ever lived, the proof was invariably marshalled with a masterly elegance. It is not until the reader gets to the occasional angry dissent that he realizes that Cardozo had been turning the law of New York upside down. During his twenty [*sic*] years Cardozo succeeded to an extraordinary degree in freeing up—and, of course, unsettling—the law of New York. It is true that he went about doing this in such an elliptical, convoluted, at times incomprehensible, fashion that the less gifted lower court New York judges were frequently at a loss to understand what they were being told. (Id.)

As for Cardozo's major nonjudicial work, *The Nature of the Judicial Process,* Gilmore tells us that "nobody reads" it; "as a matter of strict fact, [the book] has almost no intellectual content" (p. 76). Nevertheless "Cardozo's hesitant confession [in *The Nature of the Judicial Process*] that judges were, on rare occasions, more than simple automata . . . was widely regarded as a legal version of hard-core pornography," and Cardozo was courting impeachment in making this confession (p. 77).

What is one to make of this? Toward the end of his life, which is the period from which *The Ages of American Law* comes, Gilmore, having attained eminence, succumbed to the temptation to write irresponsibly.[25] It is speculation, not fact, that Cardozo thought it his mission in life to redeem his father's sins; and it is almost certainly wrong that he decided to renounce the world's pleasures in favor of a life of meditation—which, by the way, the life of a practicing lawyer and judge is not. *The Nature of the Judicial Process* is still in print after almost seventy years and has, "as a matter of strict fact" (a bluff phrase), a good deal of intellectual content, as we shall see in the next chapter. Although Cardozo was an innovative judge, his innovations were for the most part modest and incremental,[26] and with the possible exception of *MacPherson* (see chapter 6) cannot rightly be described as turning the law upside down. There were some occasions on which Cardozo—like every judge in history—concealed innovation as fidelity to settled law, and more on which he did not advertise the element of innovation, but these never provoked an "angry" dissent. As far as I have discovered, there were no angry dissents in the New York Court of Appeals in Cardozo's time— an example of civility from which modern judges could learn. Cardozo's opinions are not elliptical, convoluted, or incomprehensible; they are for the most part uncommonly lucid. To Gilmore, the mark of Cardozo's being "one of the best case lawyers who ever lived" was his ability to bamboozle his colleagues concerning the state of the precedents. This assessment is either an example of damning with faint praise or an expression of cynicism about the legal process; it is also excessively disparaging of Cardozo's colleagues, who were competent professionals although not sparklers.

Alfred Konefsky begins a long and ambitious article on Car-

25. Peter R. Teachout puts it more politely in his review of *The Ages of American Law*, "Gilmore's New Book: Turning and Turning in the Widening Gyre," 2 *Vermont Law Review* 229, 266–68 (1977): the book is "mythology" or "allegory."

26. Andrew L. Kaufman, "Judging New York Style: A Brief Retrospective of Two New York Judges," in *Yearbook 1988, Supreme Court Historical Society* 60, 63–65.

dozo's opinion in the *Allegheny College* case[27] with approximately the same block quotation from *The Ages of American Law.*[28] A woman had pledged a sum of money to Allegheny College to be paid after her death and to be administered by the college as a fund in her memory. She paid part before she died but later notified the college that she was revoking the rest of the gift. After she died the college sued her estate for the unpaid balance of the original pledge. The defense was that her promise to make the gift had not been supported by "consideration." This technical legal term refers to the fact that, in general (though with many exceptions), Anglo-American courts will not enforce a promise that is not in exchange for something, if only for another promise. As the college had promised the woman nothing in return for her promise of the gift, nor given her any other thing of value in exchange for the promise, it seemed that the promise must be unenforceable. However, Cardozo's opinion for the court found consideration in the college's "implied promise" to do whatever was necessary or customary to maintain the memorial in the spirit of its creation. This is generally and rightly considered too clever by half, yet Cardozo was plainly on to something because it is now accepted that charitable subscriptions are enforceable without consideration.[29] Furthermore, the opinion was a seminal contribution to the emerging doctrine of promissory estoppel.[30]

27. Allegheny College v. National Chautauqua County Bank, 246 N.Y. 369, 159 N.E. 173 (1927).

28. Alfred S. Konefsky, "How to Read, or at Least Not Misread, Cardozo in the *Allegheny College* Case," 36 *Buffalo Law Review* 645 (1987). Subsequent page references to this article are in the text.

29. And apparently the *Allegheny* opinion gave impetus to this movement. E. Allan Farnsworth, *Contracts* 91 n. 16 (1982). For an economic argument in support of such enforcement, see my article "Gratuitous Promises in Economics and Law," 6 *Journal of Legal Studies* 411 (1977), esp. p. 420. The argument against is that by making charitable pledges more costly, the rule discourages such pledges.

30. Arthur L. Corbin, "Mr. Justice Cardozo and the Law of Contracts," 52 *Harvard Law Review* 408, 417–18 (1939). The article also appears in volume 48 of the *Yale Law Journal* and volume 39 of the *Columbia Law Review*. The doctrine of

Konefsky regards the opinion as a good example of the elliptical, convoluted, and incomprehensible method that Gilmore
discerned, and wonders whether it may not be "frustrating, elusive, and occasionally impenetrable" into the bargain (p. 645).
Yet, while acknowledging that the opinion has frequently been
misread by able scholars—evidence enough, one might have
thought, that it raised problems of comprehension—Konefsky
ultimately exonerates Cardozo from all charges except that of
elusiveness. Still, disquiet peeps through at various places. Konefsky says that "every once in a while, Cardozo gets under my
skin" (p. 654). He wonders about the purpose of all the "'fancy
dancing'" (p. 686 n. 83). He says there are places in the *Allegheny
College* opinion where Cardozo was "totally disingenuous" and
that Cardozo may have been "capable of cynicism" in invoking formal doctrine to relax the requirement of consideration
(p. 677). Konefsky's closing image is that of "Cardozo trapped by
the facts of the case and the unsettled law, an image of a man in
a cage" (p. 687). It is true that, on the whole, Konefsky's evaluation is positive: "Bargain theory was used [by Cardozo in *Allegheny College*] to make all doctrinal moves appear as mainstream
as possible. To make such gains, in a two-front war with such
poor troops on such unpromising terrain, bordered on the inspired" (id.). Yet the image lingers of a tricky guy. And here is
Leon Lipson's summation of *Allegheny College:* "[Cardozo's trouble
in the case] was that on the consideration side he had a solid rule
but shaky facts; on the promissory-estoppel side he had a shaky
rule but (potentially) solid facts. He twirled the Thaumatrope in
order to give the impression that he had solid facts fitting a solid
rule. Some lawyers think that what emerges instead is a picture
of a bird on a horse's back."[31] This is not an admiring comment.

---

promissory estoppel allows the enforcement of a promise not supported by consideration if the promise was likely to induce and did induce reliance by the promisee.

31. Leon S. Lipson, "The Allegheny College Case," 23 *Yale Law Report,* Spring

Karl Llewellyn praised Cardozo in his book *The Common Law Tradition,* though obscurely and with reservations, even conde-scension: "It is a fair comment on Cardozo's opinions that if you do not see real and rather clear guidance for the future in them, then neither did he. It is a fair comment, also, that no judge has ever had a stronger urge to leave an opinion in clean harmony with the authorities—duly explained; in such harmony that on the point in hand it supersedes them. It is a fair comment, finally, that his mind was inherently on the oversubtle side, and at the same time sensitive to the immediate equities of the controversy to a degree rarely rivaled. What in the ordinary course, and transcendently in his best work, controlled all this was his drive to give clear and reasoned guidance for a whole type-situation and his wisdom in judging where sound guidance lay."[32] The book in which this high but equivocal praise appears is dedicated to ten "Great Commercial Judges," beginning with Holt and Mansfield, and ending with Learned Hand. Cardozo is not among them.

Cardozo's most famous opinion—*Palsgraf* (see chapter 3)—has drawn its share of criticism. The most interesting is that of Pro-fessor (now Judge) Noonan, who accuses Cardozo of deficiency in empathy, of suppressing critical facts, and of blindness to the human issues and to the disparity in resources of the litigants. He is particularly critical of Cardozo's ordering Mrs. Palsgraf, a poor woman, to pay the railroad's costs of suit.[33] As Noonan

---

1977, at 8, 11. A Thaumatrope is a device in which two objects are painted on opposite sides of a card, for example, a man and a horse or a bird and a cage, and the card is fitted into a frame with a handle. When the handle is rotated rapidly, the onlooker sees the two objects combined into a single picture—the man on the horse's back or the bird in the cage.

32. Karl N. Llewellyn, *The Common Law Tradition: Deciding Appeals* 443 (1960).

33. John T. Noonan, Jr., "The Passengers of *Palsgraf,*" in Noonan, *Persons and Masks of the Law: Cardozo, Holmes, Jefferson, and Wythe as Makers of the Masks* 111, 144 (1976). Noonan's criticisms are repeated and amplified in Walter Otto Wey-rauch, "Law as Mask—Legal Ritual and Relevance," 66 *California Law Review* 699,

points out, although normally the losing party pays the winner's costs as well as his own, there is judicial discretion to let each party bear its own costs. Noonan fails to note, however, that the briefs in *Palsgraf* contain no reference to the question of who should pay costs in the event the railroad won. Since Mrs. Palsgraf's lawyer did not raise the issue, the judges were unlikely to notice it. There is, unsurprisingly, no discussion of the issue in the *Palsgraf* opinion—just a sentence at the end awarding costs to the railroad. Without remarking that costs had never been made an issue in the case, feminists have picked up on Noonan's criticism and cast Cardozo in "the image," which "women abhor," "of the judge cleaning and polishing principles with his back turned to the parties."[34]

The most compendious criticism of Cardozo is that of G. Edward White. It is criticism of both the man and the judge, with emphasis on manipulation and concealment. Albert Cardozo's resignation "dishonored the Cardozos and created in his son Benjamin a lifetime mission of restoring the family name."[35] The "mission of restoration dictated that to some extent he seek public contacts and even covet public attention," tasks in which "he proved remarkably adept, despite his reclusive tendencies" (p. 255). He projected shyness as modesty and in this and other ways advanced his career; his "self-effacement and charm masked his ambition but did not eradicate it" (id.). "Cardozo's surface affect—gentle, ethereal, humble, lavish in his praise of others—did not adequately convey his skepticism, ambition, bitterness,

---

704–706 (1978). Noonan praises Cardozo's constitutional opinions, however, in "Ordered Liberty: Cardozo and the Constitution," 1 *Cardozo Law Review* 257 (1979). "Costs of suit" refers to filing fees, witness fees, expenses of copying documents, and other litigation expenses, but usually, and in Cardozo's day, almost always, excludes the principal expense of litigation—attorneys' fees. It excluded them in *Palsgraf*.

34. Catherine Weiss and Louise Melling, "The Legal Education of Twenty Women," 40 *Stanford Law Review* 1299, 1350 (1988).

35. White, note 1 above, at 255. Subsequent page references to White's book are in the text.

and tendency to evaluate others critically. To an extent he must have worn a mask in public, his graciousness and charity representing defenses against overly intimate contact with others" (p. 256). There is much speculation in this portrait,[36] but except for the ascription of bitterness it is not implausible. Yet it would have added balance as well as charity to the portrait if White had acknowledged that we *all* wear masks in public.[37]

Cardozo's judicial opinions, White continues, "exhibited a similar quality, and were at times close to being disingenuous" (id.). Cardozo wasn't fooling himself—he knew that judges often were free to shape the law—but he thought a judge "might choose to mask that freedom of choice in the traditional techniques and canons of his profession. That kind of artifice, for Cardozo, was not hypocrisy or dishonesty but simply good sense. It strengthened rather than undermined respect for the judiciary" (pp. 256–257). *The Nature of the Judicial Process*—a book that "is continually recommended to aspiring law students on the perhaps dubious ground" of still possessing its original validity and vitality (p. 259)—"represented a compromise between oracular and nihilistic judging," enabling Cardozo to "face the fact that he was not an oracle without appearing to be a tyrant" (id.). "Cardozo's interpretation of his office, then, juxtaposed a private craving for certainty and predictability against a public acceptance of the complexities of modern life" (p. 260). His method in writing opinions was "to lay bare the competing elements in a case and then to make it appear as if their clash had been resolved by someone other than himself . . . He was candid in revealing the problems he faced, but in solving them he retreated behind conventional techniques of judicial subterfuge—of which he was a master. His retreat was motivated less by a desire to deceive than by a fear that if the sovereign prerogative of choice

36. Bricker, note 1 above, at 23 n. 112, notes several inaccuracies in White's character sketch, all of which tend to denigrate Cardozo.
37. Erving Goffman, *The Presentation of Self in Everyday Life* (1959).

were truly his alone he would not know how to make it. The judiciary's arsenal of craft techniques was his barrier against that fear" (id.).

Against this astringent (although insightful) critique we may set the graceful homage of Professor Freund, who comparing Cardozo and Holmes says "it was this capacity to see the general in the particular that Holmes regarded as the difference between philosophy and gossip, and it was this capacity that joined Holmes and Cardozo in an unmistakable distinction of mind . . . This shy, ruminating, self-mocking, morally sensitive, preternaturally acute, large-visioned man of the law, with a kind of poet's intuition of practical affairs, was the darling of students and scholars in his own day and remains so in ours."[38] And it should be noted that virtually all the critics of Cardozo, even Frank, dutifully acknowledge his greatness en route to delivering their criticisms. But the nature of his greatness is not explained and often sounds like deceit, concealment, and manipulation, the lawyer's shady arts. Cardozo's admirers offer rather few particulars as well. There is a mystery here which the subsequent chapters will try to unravel.

38. Freund, note 19 above, at 2, 3. Freund adds, however, that Frankfurter had reread *The Nature of the Judicial Process* shortly after his own appointment to the Supreme Court "and found it not very helpful in the decision of actual cases." Id. at 3, 4. This remark reminded me that Judge Friendly, shortly before his death, had told me that he had recently reread Cardozo's book and thought it dated. Speaking as a judge, I can say with some confidence that as a handbook of the judicial craft the book is indeed pretty useless. But it has real merit as an exposition of a jurisprudential position, as I try to show in the next chapter.

# 2

## Cardozo's Judicial Philosophy

WRITING IN 1947, the distinguished legal scholar Edwin Patterson opined that Cardozo's "extra-judicial writings contain his more articulate philosophy of law, and are thus more likely to be enduring than his opinions as a judge."[1] This prediction thus far has proved false. Which is not to denigrate those writings: The best known of them—*The Nature of the Judicial Process*—is heavily cited for a work of jurisprudence written as long ago as it was. Between 1966 (the first year of the *Social Sciences Citation Index*) and 1988 the book was cited an average of 28.4 times a year in journals tabulated by the *Index*. This compares with an average of 41.6 citations for Holmes's *The Common Law* (1881)—widely considered the best book on law ever written by an American—over the same period. No works of jurisprudence earlier than H. L. A. Hart's *The Concept of Law* (1960) are cited with comparable frequency except Holmes's article "The Path of the Law,"[2] which, however, is cited even more frequently than *The Common Law*. Cardozo's other nonjudicial writings are rarely cited; the average number of citations to all of them to-

---

1. Edwin W. Patterson, "Foreword," in *Selected Writings of Benjamin Nathan Cardozo: The Choice of Tycho Brahe* v (Margaret E. Hall ed. 1947). My page references to Cardozo's nonjudicial writings are, with one exception, to this book, which collects virtually all those writings. The exception is *The Nature of the Judicial Process* (1921), which is still in print and widely available; I cite to the original page numbers in that book.

2. 10 *Harvard Law Review* 457 (1897).

gether is less than two-thirds the average number of citations to *The Nature of the Judicial Process.*

Although the frequency with which the book is cited marks it as a classic, and it is still read a fair amount, it is little discussed and is considered in sophisticated legal circles old hat. In part this is for the reason given by Gilmore—its central message is no longer news (today do we not all know that judges are not *simple* automata?)—and in part because it is considered derivative from Holmes and therefore unoriginal. In contrast to the tepid modern reaction to Cardozo's nonjudicial writings, his judicial opinions continue to be a staple of teaching and scholarly discussion in contracts, torts, and other fields; the passage of time has not dulled their luster.

The modern assessment of *The Nature of the Judicial Process* is questionable. The formalist movement against which Cardozo was writing never died; it just went into a hibernation from which it has now awakened,[3] making Cardozo's strictures against formalism (the judge as calculating machine) as timely as ever. And although with the aid of hindsight almost everything in *The Nature of the Judicial Process* can be found in embryo somewhere in Holmes's voluminous writings—Holmes was indeed the more seminal thinker—Cardozo's book, especially when read in conjunction with his neglected later essay, "Jurisprudence" (*Selected Writings* 7), is the classic full-blown exposition of the pragmatic position sketched by Holmes and further developed—after *The Nature of the Judicial Process,* be it noted—by the legal realists.

The current depreciation of Cardozo's nonjudicial writings is due largely, I think, to their style, which both is more florid than that of his opinions and has colored impressions of the style of the opinions. Cardozo's style is a focus of my study, and I begin by noting that there are two diametrically opposed assessments of it. One is that it is terse and lucid, the other that it is fancy

---

3. I discuss the recrudescence of formalism in *The Problems of Jurisprudence* (1990).

and precious. The assessments are not inconsistent. Sometimes Cardozo writes tersely and lucidly, sometimes fancily and preciously. The former style dominates in his judicial opinions; the latter is far more marked (though not dominant) in his nonjudicial writings. Here is an example—and not an isolated one—from *The Growth of the Law* (1924): "Judges march at times to pitiless conclusions under the prod of a remorseless logic which is supposed to leave them no alternative. They deplore the sacrificial rite. They perform it, none the less, with averted gaze, convinced as they plunge the knife that they obey the bidding of their office. The victim is offered up to the gods of jurisprudence on the altar of regularity" (*Selected Writings* 215). Extended—indeed extravagant—metaphor, a tone arch and coy, and staccato sentences lending a dramatic air to the proceedings—these are hallmarks of the overdone style that is common in Cardozo's nonjudicial prose, and it is to the frequency of such passages that the widespread impression of Cardozo's nonjudicial writings as musty, unreadable classics is due. This is a pity, because (content aside) there is much fine, lean, "muscular" prose in those writings. Here is an example from *The Nature of the Judicial Process*. After quoting John Marshall's hyperbolic claim in *Osborn v. Bank of the United States* that the judiciary "has no will, in any case . . . Judicial power is never exercised for the purpose of giving effect to the will of the judge; always for the purpose of giving effect to the will of the legislature; or in other words, to the will of the law,"[4] Cardozo remarks: "It has a lofty sound; it is well and finely said; but it can never be more than partly true. Marshall's own career is a conspicuous illustration of the fact that the ideal is beyond the reach of human faculties to attain. He gave to the constitution of the United States the impress of his own mind; and the form of our constitutional law is what it is, because he moulded it while it was still plastic and malleable in the fire of his own intense convictions" (pp. 169–170). The last sentence is

4. 22 U.S. (9 Wheat.) 738, 866 (1824).

a superb, in part because it is a restrained, use of metaphor to convey an important truth about law.

Here is a better-known passage from *The Nature of the Judicial Process* in which an extended metaphor is used to make an observation—about the unattainability of certainty in law—similar to that in the passage about John Marshall:

> I was much troubled in spirit, in my first years upon the bench, to find how trackless was the ocean on which I had embarked. I sought for certainty. I was oppressed and disheartened when I found that the quest for it was futile. I was trying to reach land, the solid land of fixed and settled rules . . . As the years have gone by, and as I have reflected more and more upon the nature of the judicial process, I have become reconciled to the uncertainty, because I have grown to see it as inevitable. I have grown to see that the process in its highest reaches is not discovery, but creation. (P. 166)

I have made bold to improve upon Cardozo by deleting an interior metaphor in which paradise is substituted for dry land with the aid of a passage from Browning and by aborting the metaphor of birth that follows upon the mention of creation. Here as often in Cardozo's nonjudicial writings—rarely in his judicial opinions—Cardozo is guilty of prolixity, excessive quotation, and excessive adornment. But when the excess is peeled away, a prose gem is revealed.

Cardozan prose is not of consistent quality, but it should not be judged by its worst examples, as it is by his detractors.[5] On average it is far superior to modern academic and judicial prose, and on occasion it is superb.

The substance of Cardozo's jurisprudential views is more important than the style in which they are expressed (I do not suggest the same ordering for his judicial opinions), and let me turn

---

5. I am guilty of such a judgment in *Law and Literature: A Misunderstood Relation* 293–296 (1988). I stand by my criticism of Cardozo's earthquake metaphor in Palko v. Connecticut, 302 U.S. 319, 328 (1937)—an extravagant and facetious use of figurative language, a use both discordant in a death case and analytically misleading. But it is not a *representative* use, as my discussion may have implied.

to those views.[6] Cardozo is concerned not with the whole of jurisprudence but only with the theory of adjudication, and in particular of common law adjudication. How do and should common law judges go about the business of judging? To what extent is certainty or objectivity an attainable ideal for them? What is the role of the judge's personal values? What, more broadly, are the sources of judicial decisions? *The Nature of the Judicial Process* begins the examination of these questions by asserting that the common law judge's starting point in analyzing a new case is a principle extracted from a previous case or series of cases and that the principle so extracted has a prima facie claim "to project and extend itself to new cases within the limits of its capacity to unify and rationalize" (p. 31). Cardozo calls this style of legal reasoning the method of philosophy and rightly regards it as subsuming both syllogistic reasoning and reasoning by analogy, since as generally used by traditional lawyers the latter is quasi-syllogistic.[7]

Cardozo is well aware of the limitations of the method; that he should nonetheless begin with it typifies the moderation and the respect for pieties with which he approached all problems. As an example of those limitations he instances the famous "murdering-heir" case, *Riggs v. Palmer*,[8] where, in Cardozo's words, "the principle of the binding force of a will disposing of the estate

---

6. For a good discussion of Cardozo's philosophy of law, see Edwin W. Patterson's article of that title in 88 *University of Pennsylvania Law Review* 71 (pt. 1), 156 (pt. 2) (1939).

7. Posner, note 3 above, ch. 2. An example is the rule of capture: the common law recognized only possessory interests in oil and gas, "by analogy" to the treatment of rabbits and other wild animals. The first step was to extract from the rabbit cases a rule that fugitive resources are subject only to possessory interests, and the second was to apply it deductively to the new fugitive resources, oil and gas. See, for example, Hammonds v. Central Kentucky Natural Gas Co., 255 Ky. 685, 75 S.W.2d 204 (1934).

8. 115 N.Y. 506, 22 N.E. 188 (1889). A man murdered his grandfather—who had named him in his will as his principal beneficiary—fearing that the grandfather was about to change his will. The question was whether the bequest to the murderer was valid. The court held it was not, over a vigorous dissent.

of a testator in conformity with law" and "the principle that civil courts may not add to the pains and penalties of crimes" contended with "the principle that no man should profit from his own inequity or take advantage of his own wrong" (p. 41). The last principle won—why? "Because of the conviction in the judicial mind that the one selected led to justice" (id.). Cardozo fortunately is not content to rest with this platitudinous conclusion and remarks that "the social interest served by refusing to permit the criminal to profit by his crime is greater than that served by the preservation and enforcement of legal rights of ownership" (p. 43). Here in a nutshell is the instrumental conception of law, which Cardozo is eager to establish. However, as applied to *Riggs,* the instrument is a blunt one. Cardozo might have done better to stress the testator's intent. If the testator had been asked whether he would like his murderer to inherit from him, the probability is very high that he would have answered no. So high is it indeed that there is no artificiality in suggesting that by disinheriting the murderer we honor the testator's intentions. And in honoring his intentions we carry out the principal although not the only purpose of the wills statute, which is to facilitate the voluntary disposition of property at death. Other purposes are to prevent fraud and overreaching by potential heirs—but those purposes, too, are served by the result in *Riggs.*

The suggested approach dissolves the conflict between legal policies, legitimately transforms a question of social policy into one of statutory interpretation, and in doing so pretermits a "weighing" of social policies that is apt to be metaphorical, despite the pretense that it is empirical. But this is just to say that we have learned *something* about statutory interpretation since Cardozo wrote almost seventy years ago—which is hardly a criticism of him. And the suggested approach may itself not be completely satisfactory. If the testator in *Riggs* had stated in his will that he wanted his legatee to inherit even if he murdered him, the court still, I imagine, would not have enforced the will. So maybe it all comes down to public policy after all, as Cardozo said. Yet the hypothetical is wildly unrealistic; the approach I have suggested may be satisfactory on the whole.

After the method of philosophy comes that of history. Not much is new here. Cardozo follows Holmes in emphasizing the importance of knowing where a rule came from if one is to determine its contemporary scope and relevance. He strikes off a nice aphorism: "history, in illuminating the past, illuminates the present, and in illuminating the present, illuminates the future" (p. 53).

Next comes the method of tradition. Cardozo conceives of tradition not grandly in the manner of Burke or Blackstone but in distinctly more limited terms as conformity to custom—for example, in the notion of average care that is so important in negligence law. Custom so conceived "maintains the interaction between conduct and order, between life and law" (p. 64). This suggestion of a bridge between life and law leads naturally to "the force [shaping law] which in our day and generation is becoming the greatest of them all, the power of social justice which finds its outlet and expression in the method of sociology. The final cause of law is the welfare of society. The rule that misses its aim cannot permanently justify its existence" (pp. 65–66). The term "method of sociology" is unfortunate. Although even those most scornful of sociology must admit that some, perhaps much, good work has been done in that field (I shall give an example in chapter 4), to most modern readers of *The Nature of the Judicial Process* sociology is the name of a failed social science. And since the failure lies precisely in the lack of a distinctive and fruitful methodology, "method of sociology" is apt to seem an oxymoron, or at best an anticlimax. But Cardozo did not mean to refer to a specific social science. The key words are "welfare of society." Law ought to be guided by consideration of the effects of its decisions, rules, doctrines, and institutions on social welfare. This Cardozo defines broadly to "cover many concepts more or less allied. It may mean what is commonly spoken of as public policy, the good of the collective body. In such cases, its demands are often those of mere expediency or prudence. It may mean on the other hand the social gain that is wrought by adherence to the standards of right conduct, which find expression in the *mores* of the community. In such cases, its demands are those of religion or of ethics or of the social sense of justice" (p. 72).

Since Cardozo is describing the judicial method, it is the judge (as well as the legislator) who is to steer by the light of social welfare. The rules of the common law are instrumental to social welfare, must therefore be tested by that standard, and, subject to considerations of legal stability that slow the pace of judicial reform, should be changed or discarded if they flunk the test. "Few rules in our time are so well established that they may not be called upon any day to justify their existence as means adapted to an end. If they do not function they are diseased. If they are diseased, they must not propagate their kind. Sometimes they are cut out and extirpated altogether. Sometimes they are left with the shadow of continued life, but sterilized, truncated, impotent for harm" (pp. 98–99). In this elaborately metaphorized insistence that the old, the established, the traditional, the settled justify itself by the needs of the present, we catch a whiff of the pragmatism of John Dewey; and sure enough, within a few pages we read that "the juristic philosophy of the common law is at bottom the philosophy of pragmatism. Its truth is relative, not absolute. The rule that functions well produces a title deed to recognition . . . The final principle of selection for judges, as for legislators, is one of fitness to an end" (pp. 102–103). These evocations of relativism, Darwinism, means-end rationality, and the needs of the present generation are vintage Dewey. Cardozo's subsequent (and more amply footnoted) extrajudicial writings are liberally sprinkled with citations to Dewey (*Selected Writings* 9, 24, 29, 221, 233, 250, 268, 290–292, 336–337) and contain a number of Deweyesque passages. Here are two from *The Paradoxes of Legal Science*. "My bridges are experiments. I cannot span the tiniest stream in a region unexplored by judges or lawgivers before me, and go to rest in the secure belief that the span is wisely laid." Law is a matter of "compromise, of adjustment, of a pragmatic adaptation of means to ends, of the relativity of legal truths" (*Selected Writings,* 252, 302). Related passages in *The Nature of the Judicial Process* include: "Every new case is an experiment" (p. 23).

Cardozo's extrajudicial writings constitute in fact the fullest statement of a jurisprudence of pragmatism that we possess. Although much, maybe most, of what he had to say on behalf of such a jurisprudence had been sketched by Holmes,[9] Cardozo's formulation was not only more fully developed but also clearer, more explicit, and more coherent. Holmes would have shunned the pragmatist label and was by no means a consistent pragmatist.[10]

But we should apply the pragmatist test to Cardozo and ask, What are the practical consequences of his jurisprudence? What concretely has it to offer the judge? In part, a different attitude toward the job; and attitudes can be important. In part, a methodology—familiar enough today, but this may be due in part to Cardozo's advocacy of it—in which the social interests behind competing legal principles are identified and (roughly speaking) weighed against each other to determine how a case lying at the intersection of those principles should be decided. The most concrete element of Cardozo's jurisprudence is a suggestion that helps explain his own judicial practice: the suggestion that the judge try to close the gap between legal and lay conceptions of justice. The judiciary is a professional caste. Its natural tendency is to pursue ideals, such as conceptual tidiness, that are internal to the professional enterprise; "craftsmanlike" is a high compliment in law. What Cardozo calls the method of sociology tugs the judge away from craft values and toward considerations of social welfare

9. See in particular "The Path of the Law," note 2 above.
10. *The Problems of Jurisprudence,* note 3 above, ch 7.

that are embodied in "the customary morality of right-minded men and women" (*The Nature of the Judicial Process* 106)—a kind of reflective or permanent, as distinct from impulsive and transitory, public opinion. The equally poorly named "method of tradition" pulls in the same direction.

Although morality puts one in mind of natural law, to which sociological jurisprudence sounds antithetical, Cardozo makes clear that his "method of sociology" allows natural law a considerable role in the making of law—or rather it dissolves the distinction between natural law and positive law. "The law of nature is no longer conceived of as something static and eternal. It does not override human or positive law. It is the stuff out of which human or positive law is to be woven, when other sources fail" (p. 132). The judge is a creator of positive law, and the moral principles embodied in ideas of natural law are part of the raw material of his creation. In the merger of natural and positive law, and in other respects as well (such as fascination with *Riggs v. Palmer*), Cardozo is a precursor of Ronald Dworkin.[11]

Everything I have quoted from Cardozo's nonjudicial writings is eloquent and sensible, but it is mostly very vague, and this is a serious drawback. *The Growth of the Law* admits that the "value [of the method of sociology] at present is largely negative" (*Selected Writings* 223). In deciding whether to alter or abandon or adhere to a rule, the judge is pondering community morality, weighing social interests, and comparing substantive social interests against such institutional concerns as continuity and stability; but "if you ask me how he is to know when one interest outweighs another, I can only answer that he must get his knowledge just as the legislator gets it, from experience and study and reflection; in brief, from life itself" (*The Nature of the Judicial Process* 113). This is worse than useless advice, because it appears

---

11. See, for example, *Law's Empire* (1986). This makes all the more puzzling Dworkin's ostentatious condemnation of pragmatism, id. at 151–164, and his criticism of Cardozo as holding a "romantic 'craft' view" of law. Id. at 10, 417 n.7.

to license uncanalized judicial discretion. Cardozo immediately draws back, noting that the judge unlike a "real" legislator "legislates only between gaps" (id.). But it is not clear where this leaves us; for "how far [the judge] may go without traveling beyond the walls of the interstices cannot be staked out for him upon a chart. He must learn it for himself as he gains the sense of fitness and proportion that comes with years of habitude in the practice of an art . . . None the less, within the confines of these open spaces and those of precedent and tradition, choice moves with a freedom which stamps its action as creative. The law which is the resulting product is not found, but made. The process, being legislative, demands the legislator's wisdom" (pp. 113–115).

Passages like these may incline the impatient reader to dismiss *The Nature of the Judicial Process* as a series of graceful arabesques around Holmesian themes,[12] leaving unresolved the basic question of how the judge is to decide cases that fall in the open area (and indeed how to demarcate that area). It is of no help to read in *The Paradoxes of Legal Science* that the law "will follow, or strive to follow, the principle and practice of the men and women of the community whom the social mind would rank as intelligent and virtuous" (*Selected Writings* 274); there is no social mind.

But it would be wrong to write off Cardozo's jurisprudence. It provides orientation—and a little more. For in an important passage toward the end of *The Nature of the Judicial Process,* Cardozo takes issue with the standard view, which is as widely believed today as it was in 1921, that a pragmatic, instrumental, policy-oriented jurisprudence—in other words, a jurisprudence that takes its cues from the moral standards of the lay community— must inevitably reduce the certainty, the predictability, of law,

12. See, for example, Southern Pacific Co. v. Jensen, 244 U.S. 205, 221 (1917) (dissenting opinion), where Holmes describes the judge as an interstitial legislator.

so that legal and substantive justice are always in tension, must always be traded off against each other, are never working the same side of the street.

> The system of law-making by judicial decisions which supply the rule for transactions closed before the decision was announced, would indeed be intolerable in its hardship and oppression if natural law, in the sense in which I have used the term, did not supply the main rule of judgment to the judge when precedent and custom fail or are displaced. Acquiescence in such a method has its basis in the belief that when the law has left the situation uncovered by any pre-existing rule, there is nothing to do except to have some impartial arbiter declare what fair and reasonable men, mindful of the habits of life of the community, and of the standards of justice and fair dealing prevalent among them, ought in such circumstances to do, with no rules except those of custom and conscience to regulate their conduct. The feeling is that nine times out of ten, if not oftener, the conduct of right-minded men would not have been different if the rule embodied in the decision had been announced by statute in advance. In the small minority of cases, where ignorance has counted, it is as likely to have affected one side as the other. (Pp. 142–143)

In default of clear-cut positive law, people will act in accordance with the standards of their commercial and other communities. Insofar as the law incorporates those standards, it will not defeat people's reasonable expectations, as it might do if it imposed technical, counterintuitive, little-known norms upon the lay communities.

*The Nature of the Judicial Process,* along with Holmes's much earlier essay "The Path of the Law" (note 2), helped inspire the legal realist movement, which flourished in the 1920s and 1930s before petering out in World War II. It is fitting that Cardozo should have ended his career as a writer on jurisprudence with an address to the New York State Bar Association in 1932 ("Jurisprudence," in *Selected Writings* 7) in which he gently chided legal realism for its excesses. I believe—though it would carry me too far afield to explain the grounds of my belief—that little that has survived of legal realism cannot be found, more articulately as well as more temperately expressed, in Cardozo's jurisprudential writings. The limitations of his jurisprudence are the limitations of pragmatic jurisprudence generally.

I have described Cardozo's nonjudicial writings as contributions to jurisprudence. They are that, but they are not only that. They are also a judge's effort to articulate his method of judging. In this they differ from Holmes's nonjudicial writings. Even the essays that Holmes wrote after becoming a judge, such as "The Path of the Law," are not written from a distinctively or identifiably judge's point of view. They say nothing directly about how Holmes judges cases, though much can be inferred. *The Nature of the Judicial Process* is the first systematic effort by a judge to explain how judges reason. It is also the first serious effort by a judge to articulate a judicial philosophy—by "serious" I mean an effort going beyond the standard phony judicial disclaimer (well represented in the passage quoted earlier from John Marshall's opinion in *Osborn*) of ever exercising discretion. Although Gilmore was being hyperbolic in suggesting that Cardozo was courting impeachment by giving a (nearly) realistic description of the judicial process, Cardozo was the first judge to attempt such a description and his attempt is as good as any we have had since. And here is a clue that we might indeed be dealing with an outstanding judge, or at least a judge outstanding for articulate self-consciousness about the judicial function. We must next consider to what extent and by what means Cardozo implemented in his judicial opinions his philosophy of law.

# 3

## Cardozo's Judicial Technique

CARDOZO'S BEST-KNOWN OPINION is probably *Palsgraf*,[1] so let us begin consideration of his judicial technique with it. Although the witnesses at the trial agreed with each other on the essential points, and their testimony (although given almost three years after the accident) also agrees with the front-page account published by the *New York Times* the day after the accident,[2] there are some maddening factual gaps.

On a Sunday morning in the summer of 1924, the Long Island Railroad's station in East New York (part of Brooklyn) was crowded with people who had bought tickets from the railroad and were waiting to take trains to Long Island beach resorts. Among these people were Helen Palsgraf, a forty-year-old Brooklyn janitor (separated from her husband), and her two daughters. Many of the people on the platform were carrying packages of one sort or another. Two, possibly three, persons who appeared to be of Italian origin (this is stressed in both the trial transcript and the newspaper article) dashed through the waiting crowd to

---

1. Palsgraf v. Long Island R. Co., 248 N.Y. 339, 162 N.E. 99 (1928). It is either *Palsgraf* or *MacPherson*—the latter the more influential, the more heavily cited, of the two, as we shall see, but the former, I suspect, the all-round more celebrated.

2. The trial record (but unfortunately not the briefs on appeal) is published in Austin Wakeman Scott and Robert Brydon Kent, *Cases and Other Materials on Civil Procedure* 1061–1105 (1967), and analyzed in John T. Noonan, Jr., "The Passengers of *Palsgraf*," in Noonan, *Persons and Masks of the Law: Cardozo, Holmes, Jefferson, and Wythe as Makers of the Masks* 111 (1976). The newspaper account is "Bomb Blast Injures 13 in Station Crowd," *New York Times*, Aug. 25, 1924, p. 1.

catch a train that was just pulling out. At least one of the men was carrying a substantial bundle—a foot or more long, and several inches in diameter—wrapped in newspaper. When he reached the train, the door was still open. A conductor inside the train pulled him in while a guard on the platform pushed him from behind. He made the train but in the process dropped his bundle. It fell between the train and the platform (which was flush with the train at the door level) onto the tracks below. The rear wheel of the car hit the bundle a second or two later, causing the bundle—which was filled with fireworks—to explode with a blast heard blocks away. There was also much smoke and a fireball, and the force of the blast ripped up part of the wooden station platform.

At the instant of the explosion, Mrs. Palsgraf was standing next to a penny scale that was approximately her height. According to the newspaper account, the scale was "more than ten feet away" from the site of the explosion, but the trial record contains no indication of the distance. The explosion shattered the glass in the scale and knocked the scale itself over onto Mrs. Palsgraf, bruising her. It also caused a stampede of the crowd on the platform. There is conjecture that the crowd, rather than the direct force of the explosion, knocked over the scale.[3] One source of this conjecture is that Cardozo's opinion fails to convey an adequate sense of the explosion's force. In addition, Mrs. Palsgraf's complaint alleges that she was knocked down by either the scale or the crowd, or both. But at trial, none of the witnesses testified that it was the crowd that had knocked her down. The *Times* article reports that the platform was damaged, so maybe it buckled under the scale, tipping it over; but the trial record contains no mention of damage to the platform. Mrs. Palsgraf was one of thirteen people on the platform who were injured by the ex-

3. William L. Prosser, "Palsgraf Revisited," 52 *Michigan Law Review* 1, 3 n. 9 (1953).

plosion (or, conceivably, by the stampede that it sparked), none seriously, although several, not including her, were taken to hospitals in ambulances called to the scene.

The train continued on its way, and the "Italians" responsible for the explosion were never identified. The newspaper account speculates that they had been on their way to a celebration of some sort, it being common knowledge that Italians were partial to celebrating with fireworks. Whether there was at the time such a custom among Italian-Americans, I have not been able to discover; there is no mention of the custom in the trial record or the briefs. If the wholesale value of the fireworks exceeded $10, then, in carrying them through the streets of New York City without their being securely packed and properly labeled, the "Italians" were violating a city ordinance,[4] but there is no indication of what the value was.

Several days after the accident Mrs. Palsgraf developed a bad stammer. This was the injury for which she sought damages. Her doctor testified that the stammer undoubtedly had been caused by the shock of the accident, but he was uncertain when, if ever, she would recover and on cross-examination unguardedly opined that it would not be "while litigation is pending. It has been my experience that it never is benefitted or relieved or cured until the source of worry disappears by the conclusion of the trial."[5] Professor Weyrauch reports that Mrs. Palsgraf became mute after, and—according to her daughter Lilian—because, she lost her case.[6] For this information Weyrauch relies on an article by Jorie Roberts, but what the article actually reports is that Lilian, while indeed mentioning that her mother had become mute, attributed Mrs. Palsgraf's *diabetes* to the trauma of the

4. New Code of Ordinances of the City of New York, June 20, 1916, ch. 10, art. 6, §92(6).

5. Scott and Kent, note 2 above, at 1093–1094.

6. Walter Otto Weyrauch, "Law as Mask—Legal Ritual and Relevance," 66 *California Law Review* 699, 706 n. 25 (1978).

accident.[7] This is not credible. Diabetes cannot be caused by trauma—a blow to the pancreas strong enough to injure it would kill the person, so well shielded is the pancreas by the body—although trauma can cause latent or asymptomatic diabetes to become manifest.[8] In any event there is no indication that the scale (or the crowd) struck her in the abdomen.

The likeliest explanation for Mrs. Palsgraf's speech difficulties is that the accident triggered a latent psychiatric problem that the litigation made even worse. For what it is worth, Lilian was definite in the interview that it had been the explosion, not the stampede of the crowd, that knocked over the scale, but she had been standing at some distance from her mother when the accident occurred. Roberts's article also makes clear that, with the exception of Mrs. Palsgraf, the Palsgraf family was thrilled by its association with a famous case, notwithstanding the outcome.

The jury awarded Mrs. Palsgraf $6,000 in damages (between $44,000 and $48,000 in today's dollars, depending on whether the GNP Implicit Price Deflator or the Consumer Price Index is used), and the intermediate appellate court affirmed,[9] but the court of appeals reversed by a vote of four to three and ordered the suit dismissed. The ground was that the railroad owed no duty to Mrs. Palsgraf because it could not have foreseen that the carelessness of its conductor and guard, in pulling and pushing a man carrying a bundle that gave no notice of its explosive contents, would result in an injury to a waiting passenger standing some distance away. The court also awarded the railroad its costs of suit, which as Noonan emphasizes were equal to about a year's salary for Mrs. Palsgraf.[10] Whether the railroad ever attempted to collect this award is unknown, but I would be astonished to

7. "Palsgraf Kin Tell Human Side of Famed Case," *Harvard Law Record,* April 14, 1978, at 1, 9.

8. Roscoe N. Gray and Louise J. Gordy, *Attorneys' Textbook of Medicine,* vol. 3A, ¶74.11 (3d ed. 1986).

9. 222 App. Div. 166, 225 N.Y. Supp. 412 (1927).

10. Noonan, note 2 above, at 144.

discover that it had. Although inferences from silence are peril-
ous, had the railroad tried to collect the award it is unlikely that
the Palsgrafs would have forgotten such rapacity or deliberately
not have mentioned it to Roberts.

At the time *Palsgraf* was decided, the standard analysis in such
cases was to ask first whether the defendant had been negligent
and second whether, if so, that negligence had been the "proximate cause" of the plaintiff's injury. This was the approach taken
in the intermediate appellate court, where the dissenting judge
argued that the negligence of the railroad's employees was not
the proximate cause of Mrs. Palsgraf's injury because the act of
carrying the unmarked bundle of fireworks was an intervening
cause.

This is just a conclusion. How the case should be analyzed is
a difficult question. On the one hand, there is no doubt that the
railroad's negligence (if negligence it was) in manhandling aboard
the man with the parcel was a cause of Mrs. Palsgraf's injury. It
made the injury more likely; and had the railroad not been negligent the injury probably would not have occurred. The concur-
rence of these two conditions makes the railroad's negligence a
cause of the accident in an uncontroversial sense.[11] Nor does either opinion in the court of appeals suggest otherwise. And it
might seem that, unless the railroad is liable for all the consequences of its negligence, it will take insufficient precautions to
avoid them; the costs it will consider in deciding how many
resources to devote to accident prevention will be less than the
costs of the accidents that its precautions would prevent. On the
other hand, it is imprecise to speak of the *railroad's* negligence
when the only negligence is that of the railroad's employees and

---

11. Guido Calabresi, "Concerning Cause and the Law of Torts: An Essay for
Harry Kalven, Jr.," 43 *University of Chicago Law Review* 69 (1975); Steven Shavell,
"An Analysis of Causation and the Scope of Liability in the Law of Torts," 9 *Journal
of Legal Studies* 463 (1980); William M. Landes and Richard A. Posner, *The Economic Structure of Tort Law* 230–233 (1987). All this is assuming there *was* negligence—which, as we shall see, is uncertain.

the railroad is liable only by virtue of the doctrine of *respondeat superior,* which makes an employer liable for the torts of its employees committed in the course of their employment. No large enterprise can prevent all its employees from ever being negligent. In such a setting, negligence liability is, realistically, strict liability—that is, liability despite lack of fault. Should a defendant be strictly liable for highly improbable, or in legalese "unforeseeable" (not worth trying to foresee?), consequences of its actions? Culpability is highly attenuated in such a case, and it may be "unfair," therefore, to make the defendant liable. More concretely, liability is unlikely to affect the defendant's conduct; it will only make him the involuntary insurer against a class of remote contingencies.

These doubts are reinforced by a point made many years later by Judge Friendly: "there was exceedingly little evidence of negligence of any sort" in *Palsgraf.*[12] Cardozo himself seems to have been skeptical that there was negligence, for he said: "The man [carrying the bundle] was not injured in his person nor even put in danger. The purpose of the act [in helping him aboard], as well as its effect, was to make his person safe. If there was a wrong to him at all, which may very well be doubted, it was a wrong to a property interest only, the safety of his package."[13] But Cardozo is speaking here of negligence toward the person carrying the bundle; the issue was whether the railroad had been negligent toward other passengers, such as Mrs. Palsgraf.

Let us see now what Cardozo did with the case. The first thing to note is the statement of facts, which is both elliptical and slanted:

> Plaintiff was standing on a platform of defendant's railroad after buying a ticket to go to Rockaway Beach. A train stopped at the station, bound

---

12. Petitions of Kinsman Transit Co., 338 F.2d 708, 721 n. 5 (2d Cir. 1964).

13. Here as throughout this book I omit interior page references to Cardozo's opinions in the New York Court of Appeals; the opinions are short and the quoted passages easily located within them.

for another place. Two men ran forward to catch it. One of the men reached the platform of the car without mishap, though the train was already moving. The other man, carrying a package, jumped aboard the car, but seemed unsteady as if about to fall. A guard on the car, who had held the door open, reached forward to help him in, and another guard on the platform pushed him from behind. In this act, the package was dislodged, and fell upon the rails. It was a package of small size, about fifteen inches long, and was covered by a newspaper. In fact it contained fireworks, but there was nothing in its appearance to give notice of its contents. The fireworks when they fell exploded. The shock of the explosion threw down some scales at the other end of the platform, many feet away. The scales struck the plaintiff, causing injuries for which she sues.

The plaintiff is described as standing on the platform rather than as waiting for a train; the effect is to downplay the carrier-passenger relationship (created by the purchase of the ticket) that entitled Mrs. Palsgraf under traditional legal principles to the highest degree of care. The bundle is described as small even though the witnesses had described it as large.[14] There is no hint of the magnitude of the explosion, a reticence that makes the collapse of the scale seem freakish. The scale is described as being "at the other end of the platform, many feet away," but this characterization has no basis in the record, which discloses neither the location of the scale nor its distance from the explosion. The briefs do not supply this information either. Conceivably something was said in oral argument that supported Cardozo's description; there is no transcript of the argument. But it is unlikely that the lawyers would have waited till the oral argument in the court of appeals to establish the location of the scale or its distance from the explosion, neither fact having been mentioned during the trial or in the briefs.[15]

14. There is no reference to the fact that the man carrying the bundle appeared to be Italian or to the so-called Italian custom to celebrate with fireworks—facts (if the second is a fact) potentially relevant to foreseeability. But Cardozo cannot be criticized for this omission, since the trial record contains no mention of such a custom.

15. Apparently it was not the practice of the judges of the court of appeals to

Having by selection and alteration of facts made the accident seem unforeseeable, Cardozo has prepared the way for his audacious denial that the railroad had been culpably negligent. "The conduct of the defendant's guard, if a wrong in its relation to the holder of the package, was not a wrong in its relation to the plaintiff, standing far away. Relatively to her it was not negligence at all." The reason is that "nothing in the situation gave notice that the falling package had in it the potency of peril to persons thus removed." The duty of care in the law of negligence is a duty of foresight; it is not violated by failing to take precautions against unforeseeable hazards. "The law of causation, remote or proximate, is thus foreign to the case before us . . . If there is no tort to be redressed, there is no occasion to consider what damage might be recovered if there were a finding of a tort."

If Cardozo's statement of facts can be criticized for inaccuracy, his legal analysis can be criticized for gliding too quickly over the fact that the jury had found the railroad's employees careless in pulling and pushing the man with the bundle in an effort to help him get aboard a moving train. Their carelessness is a given (Cardozo is skeptical about this finding, as we have seen, but he accepts it as the premise of his opinion), and the question is whether only the foreseeable consequences of carelessness should give rise to liability. An affirmative answer may seem plausible; certainly Cardozo makes it seem plausible. But when looked at closely, "foreseeability" slips out of focus. All sorts of consequences may ensue, with varying degrees of likelihood, if you jostle someone carrying a package more than a foot long. The package may be heavy, and if dropped may injure someone's toe. Surely if the man with the bundle had as a result of being jostled by the railroad's employees dropped it on another passenger's toe,

---

ask many questions during oral argument. Frank H. Hiscock, "The Court of Appeals of New York: Some Features of Its Organization and Work," 14 *Cornell Law Quarterly* 131, 139 (1929).

the railroad would have been liable to that passenger. If the bundle had been glass and shards had injured another passenger, the railroad would have been liable to that passenger.[16] Even if the parcel had contained a loaded gun that went off when the parcel hit the rail and a passenger had been shot, the railroad might well have been liable. What is special about what actually happened? A bundle can contain anything smaller than itself; it is as likely to contain fireworks as it is to contain a Ming vase.

Cardozo's "bottom line" is that there is no liability to an unforeseeable plaintiff, however that status be determined in a particular case—an issue to which Cardozo might have devoted more attention than he did, in light of the possible shadings just discussed. In any event, this rule, invented by Cardozo in *Palsgraf* though perhaps implicit in his famous earlier decision in *MacPherson v. Buick Motor Co.*,[17] has been followed by a number of states besides New York, but it remains the minority rule. Most states continue to muddle along with the nebulous "proximate cause" approach, which emphasizes the proximity in time and space of the defendant's careless act to the plaintiff's injury; that was the approach taken by Judge Andrews's dissent in *Palsgraf*.

So Cardozo engineered a minority solution, not markedly superior to the unsatisfactory majority solution, to a rather esoteric problem of tort law. Why then is the opinion so famous? And famous it is. It has been cited 309 times by state courts *outside* New York (85 times by the New York courts and 156 times by federal courts). This is almost as many times as *MacPherson* (381 citations by state courts outside New York, 179 within, 267 federal). And *MacPherson* is Cardozo's most influential opinion: by greatly limiting the requirement of privity of contract in products liability cases—the requirement that the injured consumer have a contract with the manufacturer he is suing—

16. Friendly's conclusion too, in Petitions of Kinsman Transit Co., note 12 above, at 721.

17. 217 N.Y. 382, 111 N.E. 1050 (1916); see chapter 6.

*MacPherson* inaugurated fundamental changes in American tort law. *Palsgraf* is also the subject of a large scholarly literature and is, I believe, the only case reprinted in *all* American casebooks on tort law.

A number of reasons for *Palsgraf*'s celebrity can be conjectured. The first is that Cardozo's enormous reputation—a reputation resting, to be sure, in part, but only small part, on *Palsgraf* itself—increases the probability that any opinion written by Cardozo will be cited and discussed more than the equivalent opinion of a lesser-known judge. To borrow the hagiographical imagery traditional in discussing Cardozo, Cardozo's name on an opinion has a halo effect.

Second is the elliptical statement of facts,[18] which strips away all extraneous details, except Mrs. Palsgraf's destination, and perhaps some essential facts as well. This economical, indeed skeletal, presentation enables the reader to grasp the situation—or, rather, so much of the situation as Cardozo wants the reader to grasp—at a glance. The compact lucidity of the statement of facts is refreshing and is in striking contrast to the flaccid prolixity of ordinary judicial prose and the occasional plumminess of Cardozo's own prose. His artistry is nowhere better exhibited than in his omission of a fact that would have assisted the thrust of his opinion—namely, the injury for which Mrs. Palsgraf was suing. Mention that it was a stammer would have made the accident seem not only freakish but silly, a put-on, a fraud. The scale fell on Mrs. Palsgraf and made her stammer. Tell us another. Great cases are not silly.

More than artistry is at work in the omissions. The more facts that are stated in an opinion, the easier it is for judges in subsequent cases to distinguish, narrow, confine, and otherwise diminish the scope and impact of the opinion. If Cardozo had

---

18. A parallel example—Learned Hand's truncation of the facts in his celebrated *T. J. Hooper* opinion (60 F.2d 737 [2d Cir. 1932])—is discussed in Landes and Posner, note 11 above, at 133–135.

mentioned Mrs. Palsgraf's stammer, later judges might have limited the holding of the case to situations in which the *type* of injury that occurs is unforeseeable.

Third, however, Cardozo goes beyond omissions, even misleading ones, and makes up facts—to telling effect from a rhetorical standpoint. The inaccurate positioning of Mrs. Palsgraf at the other end of the platform many feet away from the explosion adds to the mystery, the fascination, of the case. How did a handful of firecrackers cause a heavy scale at the other end of a long platform to collapse? At once the reader is intrigued.[19] In addition, the more tenuous the causal linkage, the more natural a characterization of the accident as unforeseeable appears.

Were the omissions and misstatements deliberate on Cardozo's part? In his essay "Law and Literature," Cardozo defended the right of a judge to deliberately misstate facts: "I often say that one [a judge writing a judicial opinion] must permit oneself, and that quite advisedly and deliberately, a certain margin of misstatement" (*Selected Writings* 339, 341). It is statements like these that mark Cardozo as our most self-consciously literary judge. But whether the factual inaccuracies in *Palsgraf* or any other opinion were conscious or not is impossible to say.

A fourth reason for *Palsgraf's* fame is the opinion's eloquently pedagogic character. Cardozo has set out to teach us some basic

---

19. If not misled. I mentioned the conjecture that the stampede of the crowd rather than the explosion had knocked over the scale. And here is Professor Epstein's comment: "The case involved a freak set of events; indeed the facts as stated seem to violate the laws of physics. How, for example, could Mrs. Palsgraf have been the only person on a crowded platform injured by the explosion, had there been an explosion?" Richard A. Epstein, "Two Fallacies in the Law of Joint Torts," 73 *Georgetown Law Journal* 1377 and n. 2 (1985). Yet there undoubtedly *was* an explosion—a big enough one to earn page-one treatment by the *New York Times*—and Mrs. Palsgraf was one of thirteen people injured by it. The railroad's lawyers did not deny that there had been an explosion, and Mrs. Palsgraf may have been standing not much more than ten feet from it. Epstein is correct that the facts *as stated in Cardozo's opinion* make the accident seem exceedingly freakish, but those facts are misstated. Professor Landes and I were similarly misled. See note 11 above, at 246 and n. 39.

truths about the law of torts—in particular, what negligence *really* is and how it is related to the concept of duty and to the scope of liability. "The orbit of the danger as disclosed to the eye of reasonable vigilance would be the orbit of the duty." "Negligent the act is, and wrongful in the sense that it is unsocial, but wrongful and unsocial in relation to other travelers, only because the eye of vigilance perceives the risk of danger." Here, by the way, are good examples of Cardozo's most common deviation from standard prose—the inversion of subject and predicate. This puts the reader off at first but turns out to be an effective method of emphasizing key words ("negligent" and "wrongful," in the passage just quoted). The departures from standard word order, and the frequent use of metaphor and aphorism, are what people have chiefly in mind when they criticize Cardozo's style as being "ornate." It is not ornate. An ornate style is one rich in subordinate clauses, parentheses, digressions, redundancies, and other curlicues. Cardozo's inversions of standard word order and his use of metaphor and aphorism make for brevity and vividness. His style is not hectoring—the Brandeisian jackhammer.[20] But neither is it decorative, florid, luxuriant, rococo. It is, however, on occasion exotic; for Jerome Frank's suggestion that Cardozo wrote with an alien grace we may substitute the suggestion that he sometimes wrote with an exotic grace.

I continue with the gnomic utterances in *Palsgraf*. "The risk reasonably to be perceived defines the duty to be obeyed, and risk imports relation; it is risk to another or to others within the range of apprehension." "Negligence, like risk, is thus a term of relation. Negligence in the abstract, apart from things related, is surely not a tort, if indeed it is understandable at all." Less is being said than appears, but Cardozo's evident confidence sweeps the reader along,[21] assisted by such minatory reminders—potent

20. On which see my book *Law and Literature: A Misunderstood Relation* 292–293 (1988).

21. On the characteristic "rhetoric of inevitability" in judicial opinions, see

deterrents to disagreement—as "A different conclusion will involve us, and swiftly too, in a maze of contradictions." "Life will have to be made over, and human nature transformed, before prevision so extravagant can be accepted as the norm of conduct, the customary standard to which behavior must conform." "The argument for the plaintiff is built upon the shifting meanings of such words as 'wrong' and 'wrongful,' and shares their instability." All this is subtler bluff than "as a matter of strict fact," but it is bluff.

With its bold generalizations about negligence, the opinion resonates beyond the esoteric issue of liability to unforeseeable victims. Professor Freund is correct: Cardozo like Holmes had the gift of being able to see the general in the particular—in *Palsgraf* he saw instantiated the basic principles of negligence law and was able to articulate them in prose of striking freshness, clarity, and vividness. The opinion is short and consists mostly of short sentences. There are no footnotes, block quotations, headings, or other impedimenta characteristic of the modern opinion (and block quotations were as popular in Cardozo's time as they are in ours). The opinion owes, by the way, nothing to the briefs, which are competent and well written, but nothing more; alongside Cardozo's opinion they are pedestrian.

Fifth, the fame of *Palsgraf* owes much, I believe, to Judge Andrews's dissent, which although much praised is inept. To begin with, Andrews concedes the facts to Cardozo. He must not have bothered to read the record, for he neither contests the inaccuracies in Cardozo's opinion nor adduces a single fact not mentioned in that opinion. After some meandering, Andrews does make the commonsense point that "due care is a duty imposed on each one of us to protect society from unnecessary danger, not to protect A, B or C alone." But immediately he concedes that "the right to recover damages rests on additional considerations," summarized in the phrase "proximate cause." Andrews can give no meaning to the phrase, however, thereby making Cardozo's essential point. All that "proximate cause" means to Andrews is that "because of convenience, of public policy, of a rough sense of justice, the law arbitrarily declines to trace a series of events beyond a certain point. This is not logic. It is practical politics." By saying this, Andrews cedes the legal high ground to Cardozo, who at least has proposed a criterion for determining the scope of liability—foreseeability. It may conceal all sorts of uncertainties, but Andrews does not bring them out, instead offering the un-principled-sounding alternative of "practical politics." (Andrews seems to think that logic and politics are the only tools of decision available to judges.) Andrews finds proximate cause in the proximity in time and space of the injury to the explosion, and like Cardozo but less excusably he makes nothing of the fact that the injury was a stammer and didn't begin till three days after the accident, which would weaken his point about proximity. He undermines his position by letting pass Cardozo's groundless statement that the accident had occurred at the other end of the platform many feet away from the explosion, and he misconceives the proximate-cause issue: it is not the proximity of the injury to the explosion that matters but the proximity of the injury to the negligent act of the railroad's employees.

A dissent that fails to land a heavy blow on the majority opinion strengthens that opinion by making it seem invulnerable; such a dissent is, from the dissenter's own standpoint, worse than futile, though few judges realize this. And a dissent that, also like Andrews's, is longer than the majority opinion, and treats its disagreement with the majority as fundamental, magnifies the importance of the majority opinion. It also plays into the hands of law professors on the lookout for good teaching cases by providing a vivid picture of the contestability of legal doctrine at an apparently fundamental level and, in *Palsgraf,* a vivid contrast between styles of legal reasoning ("legal" versus "political") as well.

So *Palsgraf*'s celebrity is due in part—but only in part—to

Cardozo's technique. And that technique is quintessentially rhetorical in a sense that cannot be taken as wholly complimentary in evaluating a judicial opinion, for one element of the technique is the selection of facts with a freedom bordering on that of a novelist or a short-story writer, and another is outright fictionalizing ("at the other end of the platform, many feet away"). Moreoever, despite Cardozo's professed (and, so far as I am able to determine, sincere) pragmatism, his opinion does not come to grips with the issues of policy that are raised by the problem of the unforeseeable plaintiff, and more broadly of the extremely unlikely accident. Indeed, one of the rhetorical skills deployed in the opinion is that of avoiding practical considerations while sounding practical, hardheaded. And Cardozo was lucky not only in his dissenter but also in the draw of cases. Even after he became chief judge, all cases in the New York Court of Appeals were assigned by rotation.[22] But we should not think that the luck of the draw was decisive. Had the writing of *Palsgraf* fallen to any other judge on that court it might well have sunk without a trace, while if Cardozo had drawn another tort case instead of *Palsgraf* he might have made of it a *Palsgraf*. To see how *ordinary* a case *Palsgraf* would have been in the hands of an ordinary judge, one has only to read the majority and dissenting opinions in the intermediate appellate court. Cardozo could make silk purses out of sow's ears—a gift vouchsafed to few judges.

I end my discussion of *Palsgraf* with a glance at the suggestion by Noonan and the feminist critics that Cardozo showed a lack of empathy for Mrs. Palsgraf. The charge has not been sustained. Judges take an oath to render equal justice to rich and poor, so the fact that Mrs. Palsgraf was poor would not have been a principled ground for bending the rules in her favor. What is more, it is highly misleading to call the Long Island Railroad "rich" just because it was a large corporation affiliated with a still larger one (the mighty Pennsylvania Railroad). A corporation is a gan-

22. Hiscock, note 15 above, at 138.

glion of relations with people, most of whom, in the case of a railroad anyway, are not rich—shippers, railroad workers, passengers, employees of suppliers, shippers' customers, and families of the foregoing. Even if all the corporation's shareholders are rich, it is by no means certain that the predominant part of any increase in the corporation's costs that is due to more extensive tort liability will come to rest on them rather than on the other persons with whom the corporation is economically entwined. Then too the large corporation will on average be a defendant in more suits than will a small one; the total burden on it may be no less. Maybe there are economies of scale in litigation that enable the frequent defendant to obtain more effective representation than the infrequent plaintiff or to overawe the plaintiff with predatory discovery. If so, there is no evidence of it in *Palsgraf*. The railroad's brief is not markedly superior to the plaintiff's, and the railroad did not beat down Mrs. Palsgraf and her lawyer with a barrage of discovery requests or high-priced experts. Indeed, the railroad called no witnesses at trial but was content with cross-examining the plaintiff's witnesses. It put on a bargain-basement defense.

My second example of Cardozo's judicial technique is his opinion in *Hynes v. New York Central R. Co.*[23] Though a much less famous case than *Palsgraf* (it has been cited only twenty-six times), it shows Cardozo at his most sparkling, has been singled out by Professor Weisberg as a model of legal writing,[24] and in retrospect can be seen as an early and prescient judicial step toward the abolition (not yet complete) of the technicalities that enmesh the subject of landowners' common law tort liability for dangerous conditions on their land. The facts were not in dispute. The railroad's right-of-way abutted the Harlem River,

23. 231 N.Y. 229, 131 N.E. 898 (1921).
24. Richard H. Weisberg, *When Lawyers Write* 10 (1987). In "Judicial Discretion, or the Self on the Shelf," 10 *Cardozo Law Review* 105, 110 (1988), Weisberg calls the opinion "stunning." See also his discussion of the case in "Law, Literature and Cardozo's Judicial Poetics," 1 *Cardozo Law Review* 283, 324–326 (1979).

which separates the Bronx and Manhattan and is a public way. Someone unknown had years earlier nailed a plank to the top of the bulkhead that bounded the right-of-way on the water side. The plank projected several feet over the water and was used as a diving board by neighborhood youths. The motive power for the trains run by the railroad at this point was supplied by overhead high-tension wires which ran directly over the springboard, although the tracks themselves appear from the photographs in the record to have been set about fifteen to twenty-five feet back from the bulkhead at that point. James Harvey Hynes, age sixteen, swam across the river to the bulkhead, climbed onto it, and walked out on the plank, poised to dive. At this very instant several of the overhead wires fell. One or more struck Hynes on the back and another struck the plank, breaking it off at the bulkhead. Hynes was swept into the water along with the plank, and when the wires hit the water there was a flash. The record does not indicate whether death was by electrocution or by drowning.

The suit charged the railroad with negligence in the maintenance of its right-of-way. The defense was that there is no duty of care to a trespasser. The lower courts agreed and dismissed the suit. They reasoned that the plank was a fixture of, and therefore became a part of, the railroad's real estate, making Hynes a trespasser when he was killed.[25] The plank was not an impediment to navigation, because the part of the river under it was too shallow to be navigated, and anyway the railroad had a good title to the plank as against a trespasser even if the state or federal government (the Harlem River is a navigable waterway) had a superior title. No argument had been made that the plank was an attractive nuisance—that is, a latently dangerous condition attractive to children. The railroad presented testimony that it had tried to prevent trespassing on its right-of-way at this point and indeed that it had had some trespassers arrested.

25. 188 App. Div. 178, 176 N.Y. Supp. 795 (1919).

The proper analysis of the case is not free from doubt. We can assume that from a functional or pragmatic standpoint the status of the plank—or of Hynes—in the law of real property should not control the issue of the railroad's liability for personal injury. Nonetheless it can be argued that, provided Hynes had no reason to think that the plank was public property or was intended to be used by swimmers (and there was no contention that he had reason to think either of these things), he knew he had no business there and he could have avoided the accident at no or trivial cost just by keeping off the plank.[26] A further point is that he got onto the plank only by first climbing the bulkhead, putting him near the railroad tracks, a place of obvious danger, although, as I said, the tracks were set back from the bulkhead at the point where the springboard was fastened. Against this it can be argued, as did the dissenting judge in the intermediate appellate court (although somewhat murkily), that Hynes's trespass may not have been a cause of the accident. If he had not climbed the bulkhead and walked out on the plank but had instead been swimming beneath or near the plank, the wires (which broke the plank in falling) would have swept down on him and killed him anyway. Stated more precisely, the trespass may not have increased the probability of the accident sufficiently to make it a cause.[27] Or it may have; perhaps the only thing that made this stretch of the river attractive to swimmers was its proximity to the plank.

Let us see what Cardozo did with the case. His opinion for the court of appeals (which reversed the intermediate court by a four to three vote, the dissenters not writing an opinion, however) begins: "On July 8, 1916, Harvey Hynes, a lad of sixteen, swam with two companions from the Manhattan to the Bronx side of the Harlem River or United States Ship Canal, a navigable

26. The analysis of a trespasser as a low-cost accident avoider is presented in Landes and Posner, note 11 above, at 93 and n. 14.

27. Id. at 238–240.

stream." The naming of the plaintiff and the mention of companions is in contrast to Cardozo's procedure in the *Palsgraf* opinion (which neither names Mrs. Palsgraf nor mentions her daughters)—and telegraphs the outcome. A further hint is the dramatic description of the accident's denouement: "the wires struck the diver, flung him from the shattered board, and plunged him to his death below." The reasoning of the lower courts is then paraphrased sarcastically: "Without wrong to them [that is, bathers diving from the springboard], cross arms might be left to rot; wires highly charged with electricity might sweep them from their stand, and bury them in the subjacent waters. In climbing on the board, they became trespassers and outlaws." Notice once again Cardozo's rhetorically effective use of irregular word order, in placing "without wrong to them" at the beginning rather than at the end of the "cross arms" clause. Word order in English tends to be rigid, in contrast to that of a highly inflected language such as Latin or Greek, where grammatical information is conveyed by changes within the word rather than by its place in the sentence. Cardozo showed that our normal word order can be loosened up without creating ambiguity—indeed, that it can be made less ambiguous as well as more vivid in this way.

Cardozo's analysis proper begins—with a boldness comparable to that implicit in the denial of negligence in *Palsgraf*—by assuming that the plank was indeed a fixture on the railroad's land but declaring that "the rights of bathers do not depend upon these nice distinctions . . . Jumping from a boat or a barrel, the boy would have been a bather in the river. Jumping from the end of a springboard, he was no longer, it is said, a bather, but a trespasser on a right of way. Rights and duties in systems of living law are not built upon such quicksands." Hynes was not a trespasser; "bathers in the Harlem River on the day of this disaster were in the enjoyment of a public highway . . . A plane of private right had been interposed between the river and the air, but public ownership was unchanged in the space below it and above . . . The use of the springboard was not an abandonment of [Hynes's] rights as bather. It was a mere by-play, an incident, subordinate and ancillary to the execution of his primary purpose, the enjoyment of the [public] highway," that is, the river. "The by-play, the incident, was not the *cause* of the disaster. Hynes would have gone to his death if he had been below the springboard or beside it." True, but how likely is it that he would have been in that position had he not trespassed on the railroad's land? This is the critical question in the case but is not discussed. Instead, Cardozo veers off to repeat that the railroad did not own the air space above the plank.

Having just made an archetypal formalist observation about the law of real property (those "planes" of public and private right), Cardozo describes the decision of the lower court against Hynes as "a striking instance of the dangers of 'a jurisprudence of conceptions,'"[28] that is, as an attempt to press general principles to their logical extreme—the "method of philosophy" of which Cardozo spoke in *The Nature of the Judicial Process,* published the same year as *Hynes.*

The opinion now sweeps to its climax:

> Landowners are not bound to regulate their conduct in contemplation of the presence of trespassers intruding upon private structures. Landowners *are* bound to regulate their conduct in contemplation of the presence of travelers upon the adjacent public ways . . . Rules appropriate to spheres which are conceived of as separate and distinct cannot both be enforced when the spheres become concentric. There must then be readjustment or collision. In one sense, and that a highly technical and artificial one, the diver at the end of the springboard is an intruder on the adjoining lands. In another sense, and one that realists will accept more readily, he is still on public waters in the exercise of public rights. The law must say whether it will subject him to the rule of the one field or of the other, of this sphere or of that. We think that considerations of analogy, of convenience, of policy, and of justice, exclude him from the field of the defendant's immunity and exemption, and place him in the field of liability and duty.

28. As Cardozo notes, the phrase is Roscoe Pound's.

No reason is given for the conclusion. If the trespass was not a cause of the accident, that is reason enough for holding the railroad liable, without bringing in analogy, convenience, policy, and justice. Cardozo had suggested in a passing remark (the "byplay" sentence quoted earlier) that the trespass was indeed not a cause of the accident, but he does not pursue this suggestion. The metaphor of concentric spheres implies that he thinks the trespass *was* a cause—for if it were not, the rule that there is no duty of care to trespassers would have no possible application to the case and there would be no clash of principles and therefore no reason to get into analogy, convenience, and other techniques for resolving such clashes. In his soaring peroration Cardozo has given no reason why the plaintiff should win. Again it is Cardozo the rhetorician, rather than Cardozo the pragmatic policy analyst, the sociological jurisprude, whose hand is visible.

Cardozo discusses *Hynes* in *The Growth of the Law* (1924).[29] He acknowledges (in tension with the last sentence I quoted from the opinion) that "as a mere bit of dialectics, these analogies would bring a judge to an impasse. No process of merely logical deduction could determine the choice between them. Neither analogy is precise, though each is apposite" (*Selected Writings* 229). In such a case, "the choice that will approve itself to this judge or to that, will be determined largely by his conception of the end of the law, the function of legal liability," and, with specific reference to *Hynes,* by "the fundamental principles that determine, or ought to determine, liability for conduct in a system of law wherein liability is adjusted to the ends which law should serve" (*Selected Writings* 229–230). But neither in *Hynes* nor elsewhere in Cardozo's corpus are these fundamental principles set forth or the ends of law specified. Cardozo is committed to a pragmatic approach that he frequently is unable to make operational so that its application can be predicted. He may have

29. Nowadays it is considered infra dig for a judge to discuss his opinions in his nonjudicial writings. I am not clear why this should be so.

had in mind as the shaping principle of law nothing more exciting than public opinion. That, we recall, was a suggestion in *The
Nature of the Judicial Process;* and in support of the sentence I have
just quoted in *The Growth of the Law* Cardozo cites a page in an
article on which the author states that "the early decisions, which
held that the landowner's interest in doing as he pleased upon his
own land, was of greater value than the life and limbs of even a
morally innocent intruder, have yielded to a change in public
opinion which places a higher value on life and limb than upon
the traditional dominional prerogative of a landowner."[30] And
that change is indeed reflected although not articulated in *Hynes*.

If weak on policy analysis, *Hynes* is strong on rhetoric (no
thanks to the plaintiff's sixty-six-page brief, with its seventeen
separate argument headings). But as the term embraces all verbal
methods of persuasion, including the emotive and the deceitful,
the normative implications of "powerful rhetoric" are equivocal.[31]
Here is Professor Weisberg's summary of what he calls Cardozo's
"opening gambits" in *Hynes:* "Harvey Hynes is instantly person-
alized . . . The Hynes narrative projects Cardozo's reader into the
familiar world of innocent boyish fun . . . We have before us not
merely a lawsuit, a dry series of issues, but a living lad, about to
be killed by electrical wires falling from the defendant's pole.
Twenty-five lines of vivid factual narrative now give way to Cardozo's equally creative description of the second implied enemy
of Harvey Hynes, the courts below . . . *We* see the large picture,
and the railroad must pay. Cardozo's opening gambits in *Hynes*
are not aberrational. They are but exceptional examples of what
all appellate judges do: frame the facts and legal arguments in a
manner supportive of the court's view. Rhetoric and style march
along with legalisms. Precedents *contra* are denigrated through
style."[32] These are indeed gambits and do not seem edifying,

---

30. Francis H. Bohlen, "Mixed Questions of Law and Fact," 72 *University of
Pennsylvania Law Review* 111, 120 (1924).

31. As I stress in *Law and Literature: A Misunderstood Relation*, note 20 above,
ch. 7.

32. *When Lawyers Write*, note 24 above, at 10–11.

unless a severely aesthetic view of appellate opinions is taken—
the "art" of judging, of which Cardozo had spoken in *The Nature
of the Judicial Process* (p. 114), in a literal sense.

It is not the *invariable* practice of appellate judges to slant the
facts in favor of the outcome, although goodness knows it is
common. Invariable or not, it hardly seems praiseworthy. It
makes criticism of judicial decisions more difficult, and it de-
prives bench and bar of valuable information concerning the
judges' views; specifically it arouses false hopes that slightly different facts in the next case will make for a different result. But
maybe I am being too critical, and not only because there is much
more to Cardozo's rhetoric than slanting the facts. I have mentioned some of his other rhetorical methods; and Weisberg, after
finishing with the opening gambits, sensitively analyzes the
opinion's skillful use of geological and spatial metaphors—quick-
sand, planes, concentric spheres, and the like.[33] *Hynes* exempli-
fies, moreover, Cardozo's suggestion in "Law and Literature" that
there is "something more important than mere felicities of turn
or phrase. Above and beyond all these are what we may term the
architectonics of opinions. The groupings of fact and argument
and illustration so as to produce a cumulative and mass effect;
these, after all, are the things that count above all others" (*Selected
Writings* 352). The more interesting point, however, is that the
aesthetic perspective, or one much like it, may be a proper one
for judging appellate opinions after all. Maybe the principal function of such opinions is to state a rule clearly, memorably, rather
than to state facts accurately, and maybe there is tension between
the two functions—as Cardozo himself thought. I myself would
think it better to resolve the tension in favor of accuracy, but
perhaps there is a case for giving priority to the aesthetic.

My last example (for now) of Cardozo's judicial technique is a
single sentence in *People v. Defore*:[34] "The criminal is to go free

33. Id. at 11; also "Law, Literature and Cardozo's Judicial Poetics," note 24
above, at 324–326.
34. 242 N.Y. 13, 150 N.E. 585 (1926). This case has been cited 294 times.

because the constable has blundered." Rejecting the exclusionary rule, the court holds that under New York law evidence illegally seized by the police is nevertheless admissible in a criminal trial. The sentence I have quoted is offered as an ostensibly neutral description of the consequence of the Supreme Court's adoption several years earlier of the exclusionary rule in federal criminal cases. Cardozo's opinion goes on to consider the rule's pros and cons and concludes that the cons have it, in part for reasons having to do with peculiarities of New York law and in part for more general reasons marshaled in the state's excellent brief. The entire opinion is lucid and elegant, but the quoted sentence is the only truly notable part of it. More than notable, it is remarkable, because it packs into a simple sentence of eleven words the entire case against the exclusionary rule. The power to compress a tradition of legal thought into a sentence is given to few judges. The most famous example is Holmes's statement in the dissent in *Lochner v. New York:* "The Fourteenth Amendment does not enact Mr. Herbert Spencer's Social Statics."[35] Cardozo was no Holmes, but he pulled off a similar trick in *Defore.* The substitution of the slightly archaic (even in 1926) "constable" for "policeman" is inspired. It not only improves the rhythm of the sentence and, by its faintly exotic air, makes the sentence more memorable; it also makes the abuse of power by the police seem trivial, almost comical. The "constable" puts us in mind of the unarmed British policeman, so different (in legend anyway) from his rough American counterpart. And Cardozo's constable is not a deliberate overreacher but a blunderer—a Gilbert and Sullivan constable whose pratfalls are unlikely to strike anyone as a menace to the liberty of the subject.

Try substituting various synonyms for the words in the sentence. You will not improve it; you will lame it; and this is a test of great writing. The power of Cardozo as of Holmes is to a great

---

35. 198 U.S. 45, 75 (1905). On the rhetoric of that dissent, see Posner, note 20 above, at 281–287.

extent that of a rhetorician—a poet—rather than that of an analyst, or of an advocate or practitioner of pragmatic jurisprudence. True, with his inversions of word order and his archaisms Cardozo violates the standard precepts of good writing. But a great writer does not write to rule—this is virtually by definition, for anyone can follow rules—and Cardozo's prose occasionally, as in *Defore*, rises to greatness.

# 4
## Reputation in General

His own little light would shine,
not very brightly, for a year or two, and
would then be merged in some bigger light,
and that in a bigger still.
VIRGINIA WOOLF,
*To the Lighthouse*

THERE IS NO WELL-DEVELOPED or generally accepted theory of reputation. The word is vague, but I shall use it in its commonest sense as meaning "widely regarded in a good light," and thus as practically equivalent to fame. A theory of reputation so defined would investigate such questions as how reputations can be measured and hence compared, the nature of reputation, and the causes of reputation—why it is, for example, that Shakespeare's reputation dwarfs that of all his contemporary dramatists combined. One reason that theorizing about reputation has not made much progress is that we think we know the answers without having to conduct an investigation. We think a reputation metric is unnecessary to show that Shakespeare's reputation dwarfs that of his contemporaries and we think the reason for the disparity also plain—he was a much greater artist. This commonsense approach will not do, however, when dealing with lesser lights (say, Cardozo versus Learned Hand) or, in the present age of relativism, even when dealing with the brightest lights. As we are about to see, the intrinsic merit of Shakespeare is being questioned and with it the comfortable supposition that, with aberrational exceptions, reputation is a function of merit, and achievement therefore the path to fame.

Although there is no good theory of reputation, work in several fields provides enough elements of such a theory to serve my purposes here. That work helps us to understand, first of all, that reputation is not a "thing" which the person of repute might be said to possess.[1] It is a pro-attitude[2] by other people toward the person "whose" reputation is in issue. While the person is still alive, this pro-attitude facilitates his making advantageous transactions, commercial or otherwise, and thus invests him with the interest in reputation that the law of defamation protects.[3] My ultimate concern is with posthumous reputation, which fosters not actual transactions with a person but influence, favorable mentions, or uses of the person's work. But in either case the point to be emphasized is that reputation is conferred by the people doing the reputing rather than produced by the reputed one—and it is conferred for their purposes, not his.

With this shift in emphasis, the focus of inquiry moves from the intrinsic qualities of a person's work to the motives and interests of the people whose activities foster the pro-attitude that I am calling "reputation." One of the concerned persons is, of course, the "reputed one" himself (whom I shall call the "reputee"). People derive utility from being famous in their lifetime and from the expectation that they will be famous (even if only within a small circle—and the may prefer fame in that circle to a broader but less discriminating regard) after they are dead. They will take steps not only to produce work worthy of making them famous but also to promote esteem for that work directly.[4] Thus it has been found that "the posthumous durability of reputation depended on the artist's own lifetime efforts to protect or preserve that reputation, survivors with a stake in preserving or enhancing the artist's reputation, linkages to networks facilitating entry into the cultural archives, and retrospective interest leading to the rediscovery of the artist as the symbolic represen-

---

1. See my book *The Problems of Jurisprudence*, ch. 5 (1990).
2. Cf. Donald Davidson, "Actions, Reasons, and Causes," in Davidson, *Essays on Actions and Events* 3 (1980).
3. See my book *The Economics of Justice*, chs. 9 and 10 (1981).
4. For a case study, see Robert E. Kapsis, "Reputation Building and the Film Art World: The Case of Alfred Hitchcock," 30 *Sociological Quarterly* 15 (1989).

tative of emerging cultural or political identities."[5] Nothing here about quality, and that is a drawback. But the authors argue convincingly that posthumous reputation does not depend *entirely* on the "intrinsic" merits of an artist's—or, I would add, a judge's—work.

Cardozo may have done some self-promotion by his assiduous cultivation of academics (see chapter 7), but more interesting, because more important, in his case as generally, are the activities of others. Often the regard of the reputers for the reputee or for his work is disinterested—the merit view of reputation has some merit, surely. But it is not always disinterested—the reputers may be promoting their own selfish interests by hitching their wagon to a star.[6] John Rodden's study of George Orwell's reputation gives many instances.[7] Here is one. Orwell's current fame rests in part on the invocation of his name in support of political causes. Neoconservatives, casting about for a prestigious precursor, seize on Orwell and announce that if alive today he would be one of them. Left-wingers vigorously contest this attempted adoption, noting that Orwell described himself as a democratic socialist and arguing that he would still be one if he were alive today. Neither side gives a hoot for Orwell; they are using him for their own purposes.

This example brings out a number of general points about reputation that, as it happens, are germane to Cardozo's reputation:

1. Posthumous reputation is facilitated by the generality, variety, and ambiguity of the reputee's work, or in short by its

---

5. Gladys Engel Lang and Kurt Lang, "Recognition and Renown: The Survival of Artistic Reputation," 94 *American Journal of Sociology* 79 (1988).

6. For a case study of this phenomenon, see Michael Mulkay and Elizabeth Chaplin, "Aesthetics and the Artistic Career: A Study in Anomie in Fine-Art Painting," 23 *Sociological Quarterly* 117 (1982) (esp. p. 137), discussing the reputation of Jackson Pollack. The most famous twentieth-century example, perhaps, is Lowell Thomas's promotion of T. E. Lawrence as "Lawrence of Arabia."

7. *The Politics of Literary Reputation: The Making and Claiming of 'St. George' Orwell* (1989).

adaptability to social, political, and cultural change.[8] Borrowing the language of finance, we may say that Orwell held a diversified intellectual portfolio. He expressed himself variously on the political issues of his day, and his general political stance was one of considerable ambiguity—hostile in theory to both capitalism and communism and in practice to democratic socialism as well. Among other notable intellectual figures whose extraordinary fame seems to rest to a significant extent on the ambiguity and variety—even sheer contradictoriness—of their views we may name Shakespeare, Nietzsche, Wittgenstein, and Kafka.

I do not mean to denigrate these great men. It is no accident they are revered. They were men of genius, but in contrast to such greats as Dante and Tolstoy (for there are famous "hedge-hogs" as well as famous "foxes") they got additional mileage in the historical fame derby by the enigmatic, in a sense unfinished, character of their work. Holmes is the exemplar of this phenomenon in law. His vast and none too consistent output of opinions, essays, and letters has provided aphorisms for every position in jurisprudence debates and has made the quest for the "true" Holmes a fascinating, if ultimately insoluble, jigsaw puzzle (there was no "true" Holmes—the facets of his thought were imperfectly integrated). This observation is not intended to belittle Holmes. If he were not thought a great man, contenders in jurisprudential debates would spend no time trying to get him

8. This is a theme of my book *Law and Literature: A Misunderstood Relation* (1988). (A notable case study that I did not discuss is Richard Elliott Friedman, *Who Wrote the Bible?* ch. 14 [1987], arguing that the imperfect integration of contradictory texts in the Pentateuch helps explain the Pentateuch's enduring fascination.) Professor Landes and I make a parallel point in discussing the durability of legal precedents: the more general the precedent, the longer it is likely to last (be cited). William M. Landes and Richard A. Posner, "Legal Precedent: A Theoretical and Empirical Analysis," 19 *Journal of Law and Economics* 249 (1976). The *Palsgraf* opinion illustrates the durability of a general precedent made such by Cardozo's suppression (morally equivocal as it may be) of many of the particulars of the case.

on their side; and he is not thought a great man *because* his voluminous writings do not compose a coherent whole. Indeed, ambiguous and equivocal expression—not to mention diffusion of effort (the strategy of the fox, in contrast to the concentration of the hedgehog)—makes it harder to achieve fame. But once the world is convinced of a writer's or thinker's merit despite the ambiguities and equivocations of his work, those attributes enhance his fascination, provide occasions for research and debate, and magnify his following.

2. Luck plays a great role in reputation. Abraham Lincoln died at the right moment—and in the right manner—from the standpoint of posthumous fame. The manner of his death was consistent with martyrdom, and the timing ensured that his achievement in preserving the union and in freeing the slaves would not be shadowed by the subsequent failures—failures one man could not have avoided—in the period of reconstruction. And so with Orwell. Had he lived to a ripe old age (he was born in 1903 and died in 1950, so with better health he might be alive today), he would have taken a position on contemporary political events, and then either the neoconservatives or the socialists would have had to disown him—he would have lost half his adulators! He *might* have offset this loss by creating additional works of the resonance of *Nineteen Eighty-Four,* but the regression phenomenon suggests that this is unlikely. And since, as Samuel Johnson remarked, people are judged by their worst work when they are living and by their best work when they are dead, producing works below one's top level hurts one in one's lifetime and does not help one after death.

3. But luck is rarely the whole story, contrary to the impression a reader might take away from Gary Taylor's fascinating study of Shakespeare's reputation.[9] Taylor belongs to the school of literary critics that is vigorously debunking canonical works of

9. *Reinventing Shakespeare: A Cultural History, from the Restoration to the Present* (1989).

literature by arguing that the literary canon is the product of forces, broadly political, that are independent of the intrinsic merit of the literary work.[10] Indeed, these critics deny that literary works *have* intrinsic merit or meaning. Taylor appears to believe that Shakespeare's reputation is the pure product of an extraordinary series of accidents, including the closing of the theaters by the Puritans from 1642 to 1660 (which by removing the incentive to write new English plays during that period reduced the competition that Shakespeare's plays faced when the theaters reopened), the variety of Shakespeare's plays (in some periods his tragedies have been his most popular works, in other periods his comedies, and in some his histories), and the spread of the English language as a result of British imperialism. The book is festooned with fantastic examples of Shakespearean luck. My favorite is the following.[11] In Shakespeare's time women's roles were played by boys. This "transvestism" was one of the features of the theater that most distressed the Puritans; so, as a sop to them when the theaters were allowed to reopen, women were cast in women's parts. Restoration decorum required the actresses to be demurely clad (by our standards), but as it happens many of Shakespeare's heroines are disguised as men and this enabled women to appear in public wearing tight-fitting trousers that were more revealing of the female form than dresses worn by actresses. Shakespeare's plays derived a competitive advantage by being accidentally more erotic than the other old plays that were revived in the Restoration—and remember that for a time there were no new plays.

Taylor's book is part of a radical-left project of making culture, and more broadly all our social and economic arrangements and in particular the distribution of income and wealth, seem utterly

10. See, for example, Barbara Herrnstein Smith, *Contingencies of Value: Alternative Perspectives for Critical Theory* (1988); Jane Tompkins, "Masterpiece Theater: The Politics of Hawthorne's Literary Reputation," 36 *American Quarterly* 617 (1984).

11. Taylor, note 9 above, at 18–19.

contingent, infinitely plastic, endlessly mutable. Everything in history could have come out differently—we might but for those tight pants be venerating Middleton or Shirley rather than Shakespeare—if only social conditions had been a little different. Nothing is fated, nothing is natural, there is no objective hierarchy of merit, achievement, or desert; white male Western culture has no intrinsic superiority; the world is at every moment ours to refashion in the image of our dreams. I do not accept the vision of radical contingency, either generally or in matters of reputation, although it has a grain of truth. Luck does play a role in reputation (as it does in history), and maybe an unearned or inflated reputation could persist forever. But the process by which an Orwell or a Shakespeare—or, more modestly, a Cardozo—accretes reputation is not independent of merit. Even though no measure of intrinsic merit, aesthetic or political, has ever been or is ever likely to be devised that could rationally compel consensus, comparative judgments that are broadly persuasive are often possible. If asked to debate the political acuity and the prose style of Orwell versus those of Harold Laski, or the dramatic power of Shakespeare versus that of Thomas Kyd, I would prefer to take the Orwell-Shakespeare side of the debate, because it is the side with the better arguments. Those arguments may not be valid *sub specie aeternitatis*—may be no more than arguable. But within the cultural community from which the debaters are likely to be drawn, they are stronger arguments than the contrary arguments.

One of the things that makes Taylor's book a tour de force rather than a convincing demonstration is the fact that Shakespeare's reputation has persisted for centuries. In the long run, we expect good luck and bad luck to cancel out, like other random noise; in the long run, therefore, actual and deserved reputation should converge. This is one of the reasons the "test of time" is so influential a criterion of aesthetic quality; time allows the random element in reputations to wash out. Cardozo has been dead for decades, not centuries, so any effort to infer quality from reputation must in his case remain highly tentative, though less so than if we were considering a living judge.

In the case of Orwell (as of Lincoln), although not of Shakespeare, about whose character little is known, reputation is a function of the man as well as of the work. Orwell was an attractive person. He worked hard, disdained wealth and position, was manful in the face of extremely poor health, refused to run with any packs, displayed moral and physical courage (he was seriously wounded fighting on the Loyalist side in the Spanish Civil War), treated other people decently, and died young. Part of what attracts people to a person's writing is the character of the implied author, and although the actual and the implied author are rarely identical, the shorter the distance between them the more credible the implied author will be and so the more popular (other things being equal) his writings will be. Cardozo had an attractive persona because he was a nice man who worked hard, soldiered on uncomplainingly in the face of poor health, treated other people decently whether or not they could help his career, and died young (for a judge!). He is valued as a figure of the law and not just for his isolated professional attainments and contributions.

Despite the stress I have laid on the benefits to reputation of dying young, *great* age can be a reputational asset—particularly in law, a notably gerontocratic profession in which much first-class work has been done by persons well beyond the normal age of retirement. Holmes was sixty-one when he was appointed to the Supreme Court, served until he was almost ninety-one, and died two days before his ninety-fourth birthday. His extraordinary longevity has added to his fame. (From the standpoint of reputation, the thing to worry about is having an average life-span!) Brandeis wrote his most famous opinion—*Erie R.R. v. Tompkins*—when he was in his eighties, while Learned Hand wrote his most famous opinions in his seventies and Charles Evans Hughes was almost seventy when appointed chief justice.

4. Taylor is correct that politics plays a role in reputation. Shakespeare does owe his fame in part to English jingoism (but he may have contributed to it as well). And when one is concerned with quasi-political figures such as judges, one should expect politics to play a major role in reputation. Yet less with Cardozo (as with Learned Hand) than with judges closer to the nerve of modern political controversy. Much of the reputation of living and recently departed judges and (especially) Supreme Court justices, pro and con, is a by-product of political struggle. Particular judges are chosen to be exemplars of particular points on the political spectrum—for example, Warren, Black, Douglas, and Brennan have become exemplars of "liberalism," and Rehnquist, the second Harlan, and Frankfurter exemplars of "conservatism." Judges may be exemplary because of the outcome or doctrines of the decisions they wrote or joined rather than because of the power or reason with which they defended their point of view. A related point is that those who take extreme positions tend to get disproportionate attention; they become convenient symbols of those positions.

5. Contributing to the sense that reputation is fundamentally unearned, a product of luck or manipulation or politics, is the frequency of inexplicable and seemingly unjust disparities in reputation. Granting Shakespeare's greatness, a specialist, not overawed by Shakespeare's fame and cognizant not only of the real weaknesses in Shakespeare's plays (unrealistic plots, loose ends and contradictions galore, frequently muddy, bombastic language) but also of the great merits of other Elizabethan and Jacobean dramatists, such as Marlowe, Jonson, and Middleton, might well believe that the general public reveres Shakespeare to excess. Famous figures often receive the entire credit for innovations or excellences that are due in significant measure to the work of others. Shakespeare, with his many borrowings of plot and character (and sometimes language) from Plutarch, Ovid, North, Holinshed, and Whetstone, is again a case in point, as is Orwell; *Nineteen Eighty-Four* is highly derivative from Eugene

Zamiatin's novel *We*. Able colleagues of Cardozo's on the New York Court of Appeals, who may have been excellent judges yet lacked Cardozo's flair, have sunk into oblivion.

The reason for such seemingly arbitrary and unjust disparities in reputation can be grasped with the help of Sherwin Rosen's analysis of "superstars."[12] (Shakespeare, Orwell, and Cardozo *are* superstars, though Rosen's interest is in athletes, popular entertainers, and heads of corporations.) "In certain kinds of economic activity there is concentration of output among a few individuals, marked skewness in the associated distributions of income and very large rewards at the top."[13] Rosen's explanation is that television and the other mass media have greatly expanded the market for athletes and popular entertainers without creating diseconomies of scale, that is, without increasing the average cost at which a given athlete or entertainer can serve the market. For example, through recordings a popular singer can reach an ever-growing audience at no increase in average cost. As a result, the expansion of the market need create no openings for new competitors—as it would if average costs rose with the scale of production—even if those competitors are almost as good as the stars. If you can deal with the star at no added cost, why accept even a slightly inferior substitute? The consequence is that the difference in incomes between two singers may be vastly greater than the difference in their abilities.

The analogy to literary and judicial reputation is close. The works of Shakespeare can be reproduced indefinitely at no increase in average cost. Even if potential substitute works (for example, Dryden's *All for Love,* his play about Antony's romance with Cleopatra, for Shakespeare's *Antony and Cleopatra*) are only slightly inferior, there may be no market for them. Now consider a casebook editor looking for a case on landowner liabilities or on unforeseeable accidents. Cardozo's opinions on these questions

12. "The Economics of Superstars," 71 *American Economic Review* 845 (1981).
13. Id. at 845.

may be only a little better than those of other judges, but the editor will have little incentive to find a substitute—why substitute an inferior product when no discount or other cost saving is being held out as an inducement?

There is overstatement here respecting both literature and law. Variety is desired, and this argues for the occasional performance of a play by one of Shakespeare's contemporaries (very occasional, alas). A casebook that contained only opinions by Cardozo would be monotonous even if he had written opinions on every legal issue, which of course he did not. So there is much room for other judges' opinions in casebooks but perhaps less room than the merit of these opinions relative to that of Cardozo's opinions would seem to warrant, even if these judges' inferiority to Cardozo is conceded.

A reinforcing point is that reputation feeds on itself. Once a person is widely known, people do not have to invest heavily to find out about him and his qualities, but they do to find out about a newcomer.[14] There is an analogy to the cost of developing a market for a new brand, which may require overcoming established consumer preferences for the existing brands.[15] Since every lawyer, judge, and law professor has heard of Cardozo, the citation of a pertinent opinion by Cardozo in a brief, judicial opinion, law-review article, or treatise, or the reprinting of such an opinion in a casebook, represents the path of least resistance; the tendency to take that path may result in magnifying the reputation of the already well known beyond what they deserve.

It may be that the continuous improvements in communications are reducing the cost of acquiring fame, with the result of destabilizing reputations, making superstardom precarious, and giving point to Andy Warhol's dictum that in today's culture everyone can expect to be famous—for fifteen minutes. But a

14. Moshe Adler, "Stardom and Talent," 75 *American Economic Review* 208 (1985).

15. Phillip Areeda and Donald F. Turner, *Antitrust Law: An Analysis of Antitrust Principles and Their Application,* vol. 2, §409d, at pp. 302–303 (1978).

potentially offsetting effect on fame in law is that the rapid increase in the number of judges and opinions is making it costlier for lawyers, professors, and judges to determine judicial quality, and this may make them rely ever more heavily on the "signal" of good quality emitted by the powerful reputation of a Cardozo.

It is also possible, although doubtful, that once a person has established a reputation, that person's subsequent work will be valued more highly than equally good (or bad) work of the obscure. No doubt the work of a respected person will receive a more eager and careful reading than that of the obscure. This makes good sense; the expected value is greater. (I gave an example earlier: Cardozo's jurisprudential writings created the expectation that he would be a good judge.) The work will be *judged*, however, by the standard set by the person's previous work, and if it fails to come up to that standard it will be criticized. Not always, to be sure. There are fads, stampedes, fashions, and no dearth of credulous observers. But a persistent illusion of quality, based on earlier work of notably higher quality, seems unlikely. Furthermore, while the famous are dazzling to some observers, to others they are the natural target of criticism. The urge to belittle is as strong as the urge to lionize, and if the effects are offsetting the famous will be evaluated, on balance, as coolly as the obscure.

Even to discuss coherently, let alone to explain, differences in reputation requires some means of measuring it. Citation studies may be the means. Pioneered by sociologists of science[16] in part

16. Derek J. de Solla Price, "Networks of Scientific Papers," 149 *Science* 510 (1965); Robert K. Merton, *The Sociology of Science: Theoretical and Empirical Investigations*, pt. 5 (Norman W. Storer ed. 1973) ("The Process of Evaluation in Science"). Economists have conducted a number of such studies. Examples are George J. Stigler and Claire Friedland, "The Citation Practices of Doctorates in Economics," 83 *Journal of Political Economy* 477 (1975); Richard E. Quandt, "Some Quantitative Aspects of the Economics Journal Literature," 84 *Journal of Political Economy* 741 (1976). Citation studies by other social scientists include Henry W. Menard, *Science: Growth and Change* 96–128 (1971), and Tibor Braun, Wolfgang

to illuminate issues of scientific recognition, these studies are germane to reputation in nonscientific fields, such as law. Such studies have a variety of uses. Consider the use of number of citations to a scholar's publications as an aid in tenure decisions. [17] The assumption is that the number of times a scholarly work is cited is a proxy for the influence or importance of the work. That many of the citations may be critical of the work does not invalidate the method or even require correcting for the critical citations. Negligible work is more likely to be ignored than to be criticized in print; and work that is heavily criticized, even work decisively shown to be erroneous, plays a vital role in the growth of knowledge. [18]

Nevertheless there are drawbacks to using number of citations as a proxy for (good) reputation. For one thing, general survey articles tend to get cited for convenience, without any implication that they are creative or important. For another, particularly well known discoveries are likely to be referred to without citation to a specific paper (Newton's law of universal gravitation, Planck's constant, the Coase theorem, Holmes's "bad man" theory of law—or even the theory of relativity or the heliocentric theory). [19] So the greatest innovators may be undercited. Recent works, moreover, may be cited more than older ones not because they are better or even more apt but because they are more acces-

Glänzel, and András Schubert, *Scientometric Indicators: A 32-Country Comparative Evaluation of Publishing Performance and Citation Impact* (1985), esp. pp. 10–17. See generally Eugene Garfield, *Citation Indexing: Its Theory and Application in Science, Technology, and Humanities* (1979).

17. Nicholas Wade, "Citation Analysis: A New Tool for Science Administrators," 188 *Science* 429 (1975); Thane Gustafson, "The Controversy over Peer Review," 190 *Science* 1060, 1063 (1975).

18. William C. Wimsatt, "False Models as Means to Truer Theories," in *Neutral Models in Biology* 23 (Matthew H. Nitecki & Antoni Hoffman eds. 1987).

19. George J. Stigler and Claire Friedland, "The Pattern of Citation Practices in Economics," 11 *History of Political Economy* 1, 11 (1979). The next chapter offers a partial solution to this problem in the case of law.

sible (physically or in terminology or notation) and provide a better vehicle for praising or attacking one's contemporaries, while the works of those already famous may provide a path of least resistance for scholars eager to save time in their research.

Also, there is an important distinction in principle, though one difficult to make in practice, between influence and quality. Given two artists, scientists—or judges—of equal quality, one may be more influential than another simply because he is working at a time or in an area where standards, knowledge, or practices are more fluid than at other times or in other places. Citations, and other measures of reputation, may thus be picking up the effects of luck, of "accidental" qualities—though there is a sense in which even the most intrinsic personal characteristics, including one's genetic endowment, are accidental, unearned.

Citations are thus an imperfect proxy for reputation, and reputation itself an imperfect proxy for quality. Yet most empirical studies of the use of citation counts to estimate the quality of scientists confirm the reliability of citations as an index of quality and rebut the principal criticisms.[20] That scientists whom we have other reasons to think outstanding show well in citation

---

20. Especially persuasive are Harriet Zuckerman, *Scientific Elite: Nobel Laureates in the United States* 184–189 (1977), and Jonathan Cole and Stephen Cole, "Measuring the Quality of Sociological Research: Problems in the Use of the *Science Citation Index*," 6 *American Sociologist* 23 (1971). See also Nancy L. Geller, John S. de Cani, and Robert E. Davies, "Lifetime-Citation Rates to Compare Scientists' Work," 7 *Social Science Research* 345, 362–364 n. 30 (1978); Jonathan R. Cole, *Fair Science: Women in the Scientific Community* 16 and n. 35 (1979); and references in Fred R. Shapiro, "The Most-Cited Law Review Articles," 73 *California Law Review* 1540, 1542–1543 (1985). For skeptical views, see Helge Kragh, *An Introduction to the Historiography of Science* 191–195 (1987); Terrence A. Brooks, "Evidence of Complex Citer Motivations," 37 *Journal of the American Society for Information Science* 34 (1986); Janet Beavin Bavelas, "The Social Psychology of Citations," 19 *Canadian Psychological Review* 158 (1978); Michael J. Moravcsik and Poovanalingam Murugesan, "Some Results on the Function and Quality of Citations," 5 *Social Studies of Science* 86 (1975); John S. Robey, "Reputations vs. Citations: Who Are the Top Scholars in Political Science?" 15 *PS* 199 (1982).

studies provides some basis for believing that such studies yield reliable estimates of excellence in areas where we lack confidence in alternative methods of determining excellence.

Lawyers are big citers, and the recording of citations is more advanced in law than in any other field. The imperfections of citation counts as a measure of judicial quality are also great. Corresponding to the discovery that is so fundamental that scientists stop citing the original paper is the precedent that is so fundamental that judges stop citing it—though judges, like other lawyers, are such inveterate citers that cases like *Marbury v. Madison* and *Erie R.R. v. Tompkins* continue to be cited aplenty. A more serious problem is the judge's and lawyer's natural preference for citing a case of the highest court of the jurisdiction in preference to a better-reasoned or more eloquent case of a lower court, illustrating the fact that law has a more authoritarian cast than science does and my earlier distinction between influence and quality. Supreme Court justices are cited more frequently than any other judges, but it would be a mistake to suppose that the least able Supreme Court justice is abler than the ablest lower-court judge. Another and closely related problem with using number of citations to measure quality is that in the American legal system judges frequently are political figures—even political symbols (for example, Earl Warren and Robert Bork); and multitudinous citations to a political figure are as apt to reflect notoriety as to reflect good reputation.

Yet, with all their imperfections granted, citation studies remain an attractive tool of judicial evaluation, although as yet virtually unutilized for this purpose.[21] They are also and by the

---

21. There are relatively few citation studies in law, and only one attempts to evaluate individual judges: Frank H. Easterbrook, "The Most Insignificant Justice: Further Evidence," 50 *University of Chicago Law Review* 481 495–496 (1983). Other studies of legal citations include Shapiro, note 20 above; Charles A. Johnson, "Citations to Authority in Supreme Court Opinions," 7 *Law & Policy* 509 (1985); Lawrence M. Friedman, Robert A. Kagan, Bliss Cartwright, and Stanton Wheeler, "State Supreme Courts: A Century of Style and Citation," 33 *Stanford Law Review*

same token a tool that can be used to measure judicial reputation, a type of reputation as amenable to the analysis sketched in this chapter as any other type of reputation is likely to be. Every facet of the analysis can be illustrated by examples from law, and specifically from Cardozo's career as a judge. As we have already begun to see, Cardozo's reputation reflects the confluence of a number of factors: the person (as distinct from his work); luck; merit; the reputers' own interests; the variety, generality, ambiguity—or in a word "omnisignificance"—of the reputee's work; and the magnification of small quality differences into big reputation differences. These factors must be sorted out if we are to arrive at a just appraisal of Cardozo.

---

773, 792–817 (1981), and by the same authors "The Evolution of State Supreme Courts," 76 *Michigan Law Review* 961 (1978); Landes and Posner, note 7 above, and also our "Legal Change, Judicial Behavior, and the Diversity Jurisdiction," 9 *Journal of Legal Studies* 367 (1980); John Henry Merryman, "The Authority of Authority: What the California Supreme Court Cited in 1950," 6 *Stanford Law Review* 613 (1954), and also his "Toward a Theory of Citations: An Empirical Study of the Citation Practice of the California Supreme Court in 1950, 1960, and 1970," 50 *Southern California Law Review* 381 (1977); Comment, "Citation Sources and the New York Court of Appeals," 34 *Buffalo Law Review* 965 (1985). Unfortunately the last-cited of these works studies opinions published in 1963, 1973, and 1983, long after Cardozo left the court.

# 5

## Cardozo's Reputation:
## Measures of Magnitude

SINCE 1982, THE CONTENTS of the principal law reviews have been computerized (by Mead LEXIS), and it is possible to make a quick count of the articles, including book reviews and student notes, in which a given word appears. Table 1 reports the count for well-known judges whose names are neither common proper names like "Jackson" nor common words like "hand," "black," or "friendly" (the search procedure will not distinguish between capitalized and uncapitalized words). The advantage of this method of measuring reputation is that the reputee need not be cited by particular work—the work may be too familiar to require naming or the point for which the author is cited may be drawn from more than one of his works.

Table 2 expands the sample by searching for the judge's name and title rather than name alone (for example, "Judge Hand" rather than just "Hand").[1] The numbers in this table are, of course, smaller than those in the first table because a judge is not always referred to by his title—especially, as is plain from a comparison of the two tables, when he is dead. Although there are additional entries, the order of names is the same except that Holmes and Blackmun change places.

Table 3 attempts another correction, which turns out to be

1. The search automatically picks up "Chief Judge" or "Chief Justice," since "Judge or Justice" is included in the longer title, just as the name itself is included. Here it should be noted that the lists of frequently mentioned judges and scholars in tables 1 through 4 are illustrative, not exhaustive; some omitted persons are mentioned more frequently than some included ones.

crucial. It adds to table 1 articles containing the last names of famous judges whose names are common words but discounts the number of mentions in accordance with the results of a random sample of 30 articles that contain the word. So, for example, of 30 articles containing the world "black," 8 (27 percent) turn out to be articles that mention Justice Black. I therefore scaled down the total number of articles containing "black" in the LEXIS data base—5,010—to 1,336 (27 percent of 5,010) for use in table 3. As the names of many of the judges in table 1 turn out not to be that uncommon (and Cardozo and Brandeis have schools named after them—though this in itself is a powerful sign of these two judges' reputation), I used the random-sample method to adjust the figures in table 1 as well.

There are a number of surprises in table 3, including the fast fade of Chief Justice Warren, which is due to my excluding mentions of the "Warren Court" (and "Burger Court" and "Rehnquist Court"), an expression in which the name is used only to identify a period in the Supreme Court's history, and the dramatic drop in citations to Justice Walter Schaefer of the Supreme Court of Illinois. In addition, Cardozo drops behind Hand and Friendly. Most important, the table shows that professional reputation in law is strongly correlated with a seat on the Supreme Court—the legal profession, at least the part of it (a part that includes many students) that writes for law reviews, is *much* more interested in Supreme Court justices than in other judges—and that judicial reputations are to a significant degree a function of recency. The points are related to each other and to the generally utilitarian character of academic legal writing.

The utilitarian aspect is thrown into sharp relief in table 4, where I have slotted in among the judges listed in the preceding table a number of well-known legal scholars, plus scholars in other disciplines upon which legal scholars draw heavily. The most frequently cited academic in the list, Laurence Tribe, is the best-known living commentator on the Supreme Court, and his orientation is practical rather than theoretical. The second most

TABLE 1
Articles Mentioning Well-Known Judges,
1982–1989

| | |
|---|---|
| Brennan | 3,132 |
| Rehnquist | 2,450 |
| Holmes | 2,275 |
| Blackmun | 1,985 |
| Frankfurter | 1,553 |
| Brandeis | 1,244 |
| Cardozo | 748 |
| Traynor | 323 |
| Schaefer | 198 |

TABLE 2
Articles Mentioning Well-Known Judges, by Title

| | |
|---|---|
| Justice Brennan | 2,201 |
| Justice Rehnquist | 1,742 |
| Justice Burger | 1,510 |
| Justice Blackmun | 1,230 |
| Justice Holmes | 931 |
| Justice Black | 861 |
| Justice Frankfurter | 809 |
| Justice Brandeis | 597 |
| Justice Warren | 528 |
| Justice Jackson | 525 |
| Judge or Justice Cardozo | 412 |
| Judge Friendly | 351 |
| Judge Hand | 263 |
| Justice Traynor | 141 |
| Justice Schaefer | 11 |

TABLE 3
Articles Mentioning Well-Known Judges
(Adjusted Count)

| | |
|---|---|
| Brennan | 2,716 |
| Rehnquist | 2,407 |
| Powell | 2,257 |
| Blackmun | 1,985 |
| Burger | 1,974 |
| Holmes | 1,820 |
| Frankfurter | 1,553 |
| Black | 1,336 |
| Harlan* | 1,154 |
| Brandeis | 1,120 |
| (John) Marshall | 773 |
| Hand | 679 |
| Jackson | 660 |
| Friendly | 551 |
| Cardozo | 499 |
| Warren | 320 |
| Traynor | 312 |
| Schaefer | 59 |

*The younger John Marshall Harlan—not his grandfather, who was also a Supreme Court justice.

frequently cited, William Prosser, is also of practical rather than theoretical bent, but he is mentioned much less frequently than a number of current Supreme Court justices, not all of whom are likely to be remembered as long as Prosser. Because the important legal cases from a practical standpoint are recent decisions by the nation's highest court, current and recent Supreme Court justices receive the bulk of the law reviews' attention. (Tribe's eminence is a related phenomenon.) Throughout most of the period covered by these data (1982–1989), Brennan and Rehnquist were the best-known and probably the most influ-

TABLE 4
Articles Mentioning Judges and Scholars

| | |
|---|---|
| Brennan | 2,716 |
| Rehnquist | 2,407 |
| Powell | 2,257 |
| Blackmun | 1,985 |
| Burger | 1,974 |
| Holmes | 1,820 |
| Frankfurter | 1,553 |
| Tribe | 1,456 |
| Black | 1,336 |
| Prosser | 1,189 |
| Harlan | 1,154 |
| Brandeis | 1,120 |
| Ely | 1,110 |
| Dworkin | 1,031 |
| Blackstone | 857 |
| Marshall | 773 |
| Hand | 679 |
| Jackson | 660 |
| Calabresi | 656 |
| Rawls | 618 |
| Wigmore | 597 |
| Michelman | 577 |
| Friendly | 551 |
| Cardozo | 499 |
| Bentham | 499 |
| Coase | 438 |
| Kant | 365 |
| Aristotle | 356 |
| Warren | 320 |
| Traynor | 312 |
| Nozick | 279 |
| Schaefer | 59 |

ential members of the Supreme Court, so they lead the pack. Burger, the chief justice until 1986, Powell, author of many important opinions until his retirement in 1987, and Blackmun, author of the most controversial Supreme Court opinion of modern times (*Roe v. Wade*), are also mentioned more frequently than Holmes, Brandeis, or Cardozo. All that this shows, however, is that in a comparison uncorrected for recency the difference between notoriety and (good) reputation can be profound. Few legal professionals would rank Brennan, Rehnquist, Powell, or Blackmun above Holmes, Brandeis, or Cardozo (not to mention John Marshall)—and a majority of law-review authors would rank Chief Justice Burger at the bottom of the list of judges and justices in these tables. Likewise in a comparison uncorrected for practicality: relatively few legal academics consider Prosser a more important figure in legal scholarship than Dworkin, Ely, Michelman, or Calabresi, or even than such nonlawyers as Coase and Rawls. Relatively few would deem Tribe as influential *in the academy* as fellow constitutional lawyers Ely and Michelman. Relatively few would think Blackstone a creative figure at all, and almost all the references to "Wigmore" are to the evidence treatise, which is now primarily a practitioner's manual.

The importance of recency to reputation makes Cardozo's ranking ahead of Traynor and Schaefer—perhaps the best-known state court judges of the last fifty years—potentially significant, since he died before they became judges. But comparison is fogged by the fact that, of the three, only Cardozo made it to the Supreme Court. By the same token, not too much significance can be attached to Brandeis's ranking ahead of Cardozo. Brandeis served four times as long as Cardozo on the Supreme Court and, although appointed long before Cardozo, outlasted him on the Supreme Court, though only briefly. On the other hand, Cardozo, having been appointed to the New York Court of Appeals two years before Brandeis was appointed to the Supreme Court, had roughly the same number of years of judicial service overall. Learned Hand wrote many more opinions than Cardozo

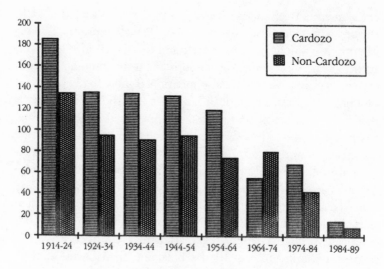

FIG. 1. Citations to 1914 Cardozo and non-Cardozo opinions.

and sat for more than twenty years after Cardozo's death, and Henry Friendly is much more recent than Cardozo. Table 4 suggests that Cardozo's reputation among legal professionals stands high when correction is made for the fact that he died more than half a century ago after serving only briefly on the Supreme Court. No stronger or more precise conclusion is possible.

Figure 1 inaugurates a more discriminating effort to gauge Cardozo's judicial reputation, by counting citations to his (and his colleagues') opinions in subsequent opinions. I use only signed majority opinions, thus excluding per curiam opinions (that is, majority opinions that do not disclose the name of the authoring judge) along with concurring and dissenting opinions. The significance of the distinction between signed and per curiam opinions is explained later. Concurring and dissenting opinions are excluded because the legal-citation services do not record citations to them, but as it happens there were few of either type of opinion in the New York Court of Appeals in Cardozo's time.

Finally, while for brevity I speak of counting "citations," the count is actually of the number of opinions containing at least one citation to the opinion of Cardozo or of one of his colleagues; thus the methodology is the same as with the law-review count.

Figure 1 counts all citations by New York courts to the thirty-one majority opinions that Cardozo wrote in his first year on the New York Court of Appeals and to thirty-one majority opinions written by his colleagues that year (the "Non-Cardozo" bars on the graph). The citations are grouped in ten-year intervals to show the effect of time on the number of citations. As a precedent ages, the number of citations to it can be expected to fall, other things being equal. Often they are not. If the number of decisions is growing over time, the demand for old precedents may rise—there is a larger "market" for them. But since figure 1 compares precedents created in the same year, only comparative depreciation is significant, and for that it is unnecessary to correct for the fact that the number of New York state court decisions has been growing. The comparison group of non-Cardozo opinions was selected by an adequately random procedure: it is simply the set of majority opinions that appear next in the reports after Cardozo's opinions. In effect each opinion by Cardozo is paired with a randomly selected opinion by one of his colleagues.

Even though 1914 was Cardozo's first year on the court and his prior judicial experience had been limited to one month as a trial judge, and even though decisions were assigned to judges of the New York Court of Appeals in rotation, so that Cardozo had no control over the decisions he was assigned, Cardozo's decisions that year are cited considerably more often than those of his colleagues, all of whom were more experienced judges than he. What is more, the pattern of citations is established in his first decade, long before his reputation received any boost from appointment to the Supreme Court.

The pattern is similar but more pronounced—perhaps reflecting Cardozo's acquisition of judicial experience—in the subsequent years that I have examined, 1918, 1921, 1922, 1924, and 1928, a representative though not quite random scatter, weighted to the early years to minimize any possible Supreme Court "halo" effect. Figure 2 pools the results for those years plus 1914. Because the citations are to decisions decided in different years, the decades do not coincide; moreover, the last "decade" varies in length from fifteen years (for citations to the 1914 decisions) to one year (for citations to the 1928 decisions). But these irregularities are of no importance, since my only interest is in comparing Cardozo's performance with that of his colleagues.

The results in figure 2 are dramatic. In this large sample of 142 Cardozo opinions—more than 25 percent of the majority opinions that he wrote for the New York Court of Appeals—and the same number of non-Cardozo opinions, Cardozo's opinions are cited substantially more often than those of his colleagues. And as is evident from figure 3, which charts the ratio of citations to Cardozo opinions to citations to the non-Cardozo sample,

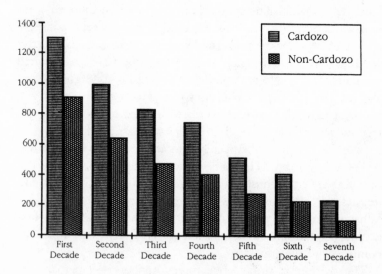

FIG. 2. Pooled citations to Cardozo and non-Cardozo opinions.

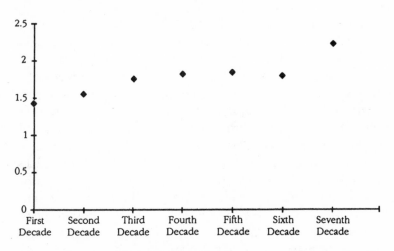

FIG. 3. Ratio of Cardozo to non-Cardozo opinions, by decade.

Cardozo's opinions have more staying power than those of his colleagues—they depreciate less rapidly.

For the entire sample, the ratio of first-decade citations to Cardozo opinions to first-decade citations to his colleagues' opinions is 1.43 to 1. To test for a Supreme Court halo effect,[2] we can compare this figure to the ratio of citations in the first decades of opinions decided no later than 1922 (ten years before Cardozo's appointment to the Supreme Court). It is lower, 1.38 to 1 versus 1.43 to 1, but the difference is slight, suggesting that the halo effect may also be slight, and possibly nonexistent; Cardozo's opinions may just wear better.

So far I have been looking only at citations by New York courts to the opinions of Cardozo and his colleagues. Citations by courts

2. What Robert Merton calls the "Matthew Effect" (from *Matthew* 13:12: "For whosoever hath, to him shall be given, and he shall have more abundance"). Robert K. Merton, *The Sociology of Science: Theoretical and Empirical Investigations* 439 (Norman W. Storer ed. 1973). See also Jonathan R. Cole and Stephen Cole, *Social Stratification in Science*, ch. 7 (1973).

in other states are a particularly good test of comparative reputation, since those courts are not bound by New York decisions as authority but will cite them only to the extent that the judges find them persuasive. Stated differently, the "superstar" phenomenon is much more likely to be at work in citations to decisions that are not authority in the citing court, for there is far more substitutability within the class of nonauthoritative citations. New York courts have cited the 142 Cardozo opinions in the full sample a total of 5,064 times. Other state courts have cited them a total of 2,777 times. Since there are forty-nine other states, this is dramatic evidence that, even in the case of a judge as well known as Cardozo, the preference for own-state precedents is very great. But Cardozo's colleagues, authors of 142 opinions contemporaneous with Cardozo's, have been cited only 390 times by other state courts. So while the ratio of citations to Cardozo to citations to his colleagues is 1.65 to 1 in New York, it is 7.12 to 1 outside New York. This is impressive evidence of the magnitude of Cardozo's judicial reputation. Similarly, although a little less dramatically, federal courts have cited the Cardozo opinions in my sample 1,112 times, versus 334 citations to the opinions of his colleagues—a ratio of 3.33 to 1.

The evidence presented thus far suffers from a serious flaw. The comparison is between Cardozo and the average of his colleagues, and this is consistent with the hypothesis that one, or even more than one, of his colleagues outperformed Cardozo on the various measures I have used. It all depends on the variance in performance among the other judges. We shall see shortly that the two colleagues of Cardozo whose opinions are reprinted most frequently in casebooks (though much less frequently than Cardozo's opinions) are Frederick Crane and Cuthbert Pound. So they are natural choices to compare with Cardozo. Citation analysis, however, does not support the hypothesis that either Crane or Pound was a Cardozo.

Table 5 compares citations to Cardozo, Crane, and Pound by (1) New York courts, (2) other state courts, and (3) federal courts

TABLE 5

Comparison of Cardozo, Crane, and Pound,
1918 and 1928

| Citing Courts | Cardozo | Crane | Pound |
|---|---|---|---|
| N.Y. | 2,173 | 1,431 | 1,369 |
| Other states | 1,887 | 152 | 163 |
| Federal | 579 | 164 | 70 |

for the years 1918 and 1928 (I have pooled the results for these two years). As expected, Cardozo's dominance is most pronounced in a comparison of citations to his and to his colleagues' decisions by courts other than in New York, whether other state courts or federal courts. The fact that Crane and Pound were indeed highly respected judges makes the figures in this table particularly striking. Consider the following passage from the biography of Crane in the *Dictionary of American Biography:* "During his more than two decades on the Court of Appeals, Crane acquired a reputation as a judge of stature alongside such respected colleagues as Frank Harris Hiscock, Benjamin Cardozo, and Cuthbert W. Pound. In 1934, anticipating his promotion to the chief judgeship [in succession to Pound], the *New York Times* proclaimed it 'a worthy—one would almost say apostolic—succession in this high judicial office.'"[3]

One difference between this table and the previous comparisons is that I have included *all* of Crane's and Pound's opinions in the two years studied, along with all of Cardozo's as in the previous tables; and Cardozo wrote more opinions than either Crane or Pound did in those years—sixty-eight to Crane's fifty-six and Pound's fifty-two. Should the results of the citation comparison be presented in average terms, as in the previous graphs

3. Stephen Botein, "Frederick Crane," in *Dictionary of American Biography,* supp. 4, 1946–1950, at 190 (1974).

TABLE 6

Comparison of Cardozo, Crane, and Pound,
1918 and 1928, Citations per Opinion

| Citing Courts | Cardozo | Crane | Pound |
|---|---|---|---|
| N.Y. | 32.0 | 25.6 | 26.3 |
| Other states | 27.8 | 2.7 | 3.1 |
| Federal | 8.5 | 2.9 | 1.4 |

(where the same number of Cardozo and non-Cardozo opinions was compared), or, as in table 5, in total terms? I think the latter is more illuminating; otherwise Cardozo is penalized for a greater output of signed majority opinions. If this is right, the earlier comparisons understated Cardozo's superiority to his colleagues, for I believe he always wrote more such opinions than they did. But even if the figures in table 5 are restated in average terms, as I have done in table 6, Cardozo continues to dominate, especially in citations by courts other than New York state courts.

How is it, in a system of opinion assignment by rotation, that Cardozo wrote more than his proportionate share of majority opinions? The answer appears to lie in the fact that many of the appeals to the New York Court of Appeals were decided by brief per curiam opinions, usually consisting of nothing more than a statement of the case and a one-sentence announcement of the result, and that the judge who was assigned to write the opinion had the option of writing a signed opinion or a brief per curiam. Apparently Cardozo was more likely than his colleagues to choose the first option, no doubt because he saw more potential in the cases. But this meant he worked harder and produced more: a signed opinion—constituting a complete statement of facts and reasons—requires more effort and has greater precedential significance than a brief per curiam. It is a fair inference that Cardozo's output exceeded that of any of his colleagues.

With figure 4 we turn to Cardozo's performance on the Su-

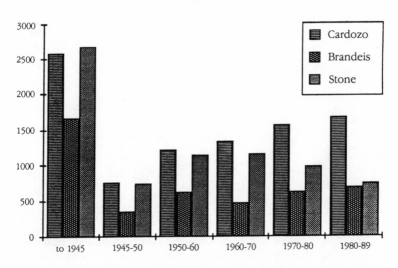

FIG. 4. Citations to Cardozo, Brandeis, and Stone opinions, 1932–1938.

preme Court. He wrote 127 majority opinions in his six years on the Court, and the graph compares the number of citations to those opinions (in all federal courts) with the number of citations to the opinions of his best-known, most highly regarded colleagues, Brandeis and Stone, written during Cardozo's tenures. The results in this graph will surely surprise. In every period, Cardozo's opinions are cited more heavily than Brandeis's, even though Cardozo was the junior justice and Brandeis one of the most senior. True, Brandeis was elderly, but Cardozo was in poor health. The gap widens with time, moreover, and over time Cardozo also comes to dominate Stone.

Figure 5 compares the three justices on an average, as distinct from total, basis. The results are less striking, because Cardozo (continuing the pattern he had established in the New York Court of Appeals) wrote more opinions than either of the others, but they do give Cardozo the edge over Brandeis and an edge over Stone since 1970. To repeat a previous point, it is by no means clear that this graph presents a more illuminating comparison than the previous one, since Cardozo's superior produc-

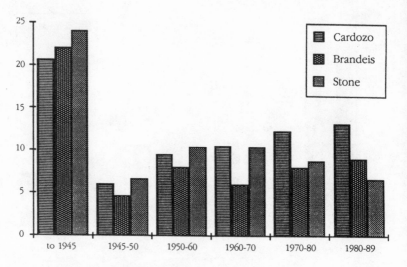

FIG. 5. Average number of citations to Cardozo, Brandeis, and Stone opinions.

tivity to that of Brandeis and Stone, as proxied by the larger number of majority opinions he wrote, is a valid factor in measuring judicial quality.

Thus far I have been assuming that Brandeis and Stone are the proper justices to compare to Cardozo—that if any of his contemporary justices would do better in the reputation market, it would be them. I test this assumption, with surprising results, in figure 6. This graph compares the average number of citations to Cardozo's opinions to the average number of citations to a random sample of opinions by other justices of the Supreme Court during Cardozo's service on the Court. The sample was selected by taking the next opinion in the *United States Reports* after every fourth Cardozo opinion, a total of thirty-two. The figure shows Cardozo outcited by the average justice—and since we know that Stone and especially Brandeis were outcited by Cardozo, this may seem to imply that Stone and Brandeis, as

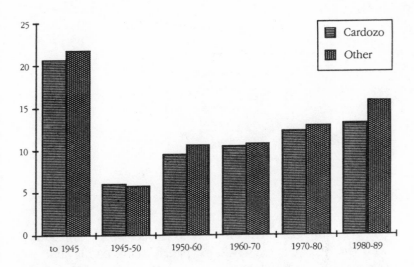

FIG. 6. Average number of citations to Cardozo and other Supreme Court opinions, 1932–1938.

well as Cardozo, were below-average justices. More likely it is a sign of the limitations of citation analysis. Cardozo, Brandeis, and Stone were out of step with the majority of the Court, and as a result were not assigned a proportionate number of important majority opinions. What is significant is that within the pariah group, Cardozo did better than his distinguished associates.

Furthermore, if we compare Cardozo's performance on the Supreme Court with that of the average justice in terms not of number of citations by federal courts but of number of citations by state courts, he clearly dominates: 34.75 citations to 20.16. And it is readily inferable from figure 6 that Cardozo dominates the average justice if federal court citations are added to state court citations. The exact totals are 106.7 federal and state citations to the average Cardozo opinion versus 97.91 federal and state citations to the average opinion of the other justices. The margin is much smaller than in the New York Court of Appeals,

TABLE 7
Opinions in Contracts and Torts Casebooks

| | |
|---|---|
| Cardozo | 64 |
| Crane | 10 |
| Pound | 9 |
| Kellogg | 7 |
| Andrews | 5 |
| Seabury | 2 |
| Lehman | 2 |
| Chase | 1 |

but it is still impressive when one considers what I am calling with some exaggeration Cardozo's "pariah" status on the Supreme Court and his having been the most junior justice for almost the entire period of his service on the Court.

The last step in my quantitative analysis of judicial reputation is an effort to measure Cardozo's reputation among casebook editors. An examination of eight current contracts casebooks and nine current torts casebooks (excluding my own) reveals a total of 64 opinions by Cardozo, an average of 3.76 per book (the average number of cases reprinted in the books is 180), compared to 36 opinions by his colleagues on the New York Court of Appeals, during the period in which Cardozo served on that court. Table 7 lists the opinions by judge.

This table provides a clue to the earlier question of the variance in quality among judges of the New York Court of Appeals. Crane and Pound do well, but the ratio of Cardozo opinions to their opinions is extremely high. And if one looks at Cardozo's colleagues *en gross,* the average number of their opinions deemed worthy of inclusion in contracts or torts casebooks is only 4.95,[4]

4. The court of appeals had only 7 regular members during the period of Cardozo's service on it. But when the temporary judges are included (see chapter 1), the average number of judges on the court rises to 8.28. One of these, of course,

which translates into a ratio of Cardozo opinions to that of his average colleague of almost 13 to 1. This is almost eight times the ratio of New York citations to Cardozo opinions to citations to his colleagues' opinions and is almost twice the ratio of citations by courts of other states—showing that Cardozo is indeed an academics' darling and providing additional evidence of the magnitude of his reputation.

The evidence is subject to two caveats. First, opinions are selected for inclusion in casebooks for their teachability as well as for their intrinsic merit or their influence. Second, torts and contracts are the fields of Cardozo's greatest eminence, and it is possible that in other fields his colleagues would shine more brightly than they do in his fields of preeminence. To test this hypothesis I examined a dozen randomly selected current casebooks on evidence, property, remedies, criminal law, conflict of laws, and legal method. The sample contains a total of fourteen opinions from the New York Court of Appeals during Cardozo's tenure on it, and nine of them were by Cardozo. By the method used above (see note 4), this translates into a ratio of Cardozo opinions to those of his average colleague of 13 to 1—the same ratio as in the tort and contract casebooks.

The evidence examined in this chapter is not conclusive, but it tends to confirm the high repute in which, by casual impression, Cardozo is held. It makes more urgent the search for the causes of his reputation. I have given clues in this chapter and the preceding one but will defer a full examination of the question until I have completed my examination of his judicial performance in the next chapter.

---

was Cardozo, so I divide 36 by 7.28 to get the average number of opinions per colleague of Cardozo. My source for the number of judges on the court of appeals is the list of judges in the front of the volumes of *New York Reports* for the years 1914 through 1931 (Cardozo sat for only two months in 1932 before resigning to join the Supreme Court).

# 6

## Cardozo's Judicial Contribution

CHAPTER 3 SUGGESTED that the explanation for Cardozo's immense reputation might lie in his gift for the compendious, arresting summary ("The criminal is to go free because the constable has blundered"), in his knack for broadening the applicability of his decisions by selective presentation of the facts (*Palsgraf*), and in his brevity and (underrated) lucidity. Here I want both to examine more of his opinions and to suggest qualities of a more substantive nature in those opinions, which show him carrying through on the project adumbrated in *The Nature of the Judicial Process* of making law more pragmatic. I will have to get a bit more technical here, but I hope to carry the non-lawyer reader with me.

I begin with one of Cardozo's best-known contract cases, *Wood v. Duff-Gordon.* [1] Lady Duff-Gordon, a dress designer, granted Wood the exclusive right to sell, and license others to sell, her designs. He promised her half the profits from any sales or licenses. His suit charged that she had broken the contract by granting others rights in her designs. Her defense was that there was no "consideration" to support, and thereby make enforceable, her promise of an exclusive right to market and license her designs. (Recall from chapter 1 that, in general, a promise is not legally enforceable unless it is in exchange for something—which

---

1. 222 N.Y. 88, 118 N.E. 214 (1917). This case has a colorful background in Lady Duff-Gordon's extraordinary career. Walter F. Pratt, Jr., "American Contract Law at the Turn of the Century," 39 *South Carolina Law Review* 415, 420–423 (1988).

can be another promise.) Wood had not promised to market her designs; he had merely promised to split the profits with her if he did market them. Cardozo's opinion for the court found, however, an implied promise by Wood to use reasonable efforts ("best efforts," in modern contract jargon) to market Duff-Gordon's designs.[2] "We are not to suppose that one party was to be placed at the mercy of the other . . . [Under the terms of compensation,] unless he gave his efforts, she could never get anything." Cardozo is not put off by the absence of the *form* of a contract: an exchange of promises or an exchange of a promise for an immediate payment, whether of cash, goods, or services. It is enough for him that he is confident Duff-Gordon would not have given Wood an *exclusive* right to market her designs without an understanding by both parties that he would not just sit on his duff. It is conceivable, of course, that she was compensated for leaving him free of legal coercion to perform—perhaps her share of the profits was larger than it would otherwise have been. But Wood did not make this argument. Nor did he argue that his conditional promise—to split the profits with her if he marketed her designs successfully—was sufficient consideration to support her promise of an exclusive right.

What Cardozo is doing in this characteristic opinion is trying to make the law track lay understanding rather than force lay persons to conform their transactions to rigid legal categories, such as "contract." The legal category is made flexible to embrace the commercial practices of the community (Cardozo's "method of tradition") rather than the practices being truncated to fit preexisting legal concepts. This rejection of essentialism—this making concepts serve human need—is characteristic of pragmatism.

In invoking "lay understanding" and "community," I am not suggesting that the proper way to formulate the doctrines of con-

---

2. The resemblance to Cardozo's analysis in the *Allegheny College* case, discussed in chapter 1, is unmistakable; but the imputation of an implied promise is far more plausible in *Wood* than in *Allegheny College*.

tract law is to describe a transaction to the proverbial man on the street and ask him whether he thinks a court should enforce it. The relevant lay understanding, the relevant community, is that of the group of people whose practices the law is regulating. If it is a group of merchants, then it is the customs, expectations, practices, usages of those merchants that ought to guide the formulation of legal doctrine. Guide—not dictate. There are a variety of good institutional reasons for the law's departing from lay understandings; it is those reasons that generate the ineradicable tension between formal and substantive justice. In particular, lay understanding is insensitive to the costs and uncertainties of the legal process, costs and uncertainties which lead courts and legislatures to create rules that make an imperfect fit with the underlying policies yet that may on balance be superior to vague standards. Still, the understanding of the relevant lay community is not only the proper starting point in formulating legal doctrine; it is also a benchmark for evaluating that doctrine. Any gross divergence between the benchmark and the legal rule calls for explanation, and perhaps for reexamination of the rule.

The approach sketched here—the approach that animates Cardozo's contract opinions and many of his tort opinions as well—sees law as facilitative rather than as constitutive; as a service to lay communities in the achievement of those communities' self-chosen ends rather than as a norm imposed on those communities in the service of a higher end. Today, with markets and private ordering controversial in Western intellectual circles, the facilitative conception of law has itself become controversial, although it remains clearly dominant in contract law. Its instrumental cast marks it as pragmatic, although some versions of pragmatism are associated with a transformative conception of human activity to which a constitutive conception of law would be more congenial.

Let us rise out of these deep waters and return to the smooth surface that is Cardozo's opinion in *Wood v. Duff-Gordon*. It has been suggested that, in beginning the opinion "The defendant

[Lady Duff-Gordon] *styles* herself 'a creator of fashions'" (emphasis added), Cardozo has subtly loaded the dice against the defendant by implying that she may be a phony.[3] Maybe; but the procedural setting of the case must be considered. The lower courts had decided it on the defendant's motion to dismiss the complaint for failure to state a claim. There had been no trial or other factual inquiry. The only facts, therefore, were those alleged by the plaintiff. The plaintiff had attached to his complaint the contract between himself and Lady Duff-Gordon, and there we read that "the said Lucy, Lady Duff-Gordon, occupies a unique and high position as a creator of fashions in America, England and France." It is a fair characterization of the contract that in it Lady Duff-Gordon styles herself "a creator of fashions." Cardozo is merely quoting a clause of the contract undoubtedly drafted by Lady Duff-Gordon or her lawyer. We know from chapter 3 that Cardozo was not completely above the tricks he is accused of here; only here the accusation seems unwarranted.

Turning from rhetoric to substance, we may note that a bolder judge, in *Wood* as in *Allegheny College,* might have forgone a search for consideration—might have upheld the plaintiff's claim on the forthright ground that the parties had expected the defendant's promise of an exclusive right to be legally enforceable. But this bolder judge would not have commanded a majority for his position. It was ever Cardozo's way, as it has been the common law's way, to work incrementally toward the goal of freeing the law from arbitrary restrictions on liability. A frontal assault almost certainly would have failed. Cardozo was not Quixote.

Had he gone his own way, moreover, we would be deprived of the most influential part of the opinion, the imputation to Wood of an implied undertaking to use reasonable efforts to promote

---

3. Karl N. Llewellyn, "A Lecture on Appellate Advocacy," 29 *University of Chicago Law Review* 627, 637 (1962); Mary Joe Frug, "Re-Reading Contracts: A Feminist Analysis of a Contracts Casebook," 34 *American University Law Review* 1065, 1084 n. 66 (1985). I find it odd that feminists should pick on Cardozo—the least macho of eminent judges.

Duff-Gordon's designs. The imputation is plausible. Certainly Duff-Gordon should have been entitled to terminate the contract without liability if Wood failed to promote her designs, and this implies that she could also have sued him for the damages caused by such failure. This conclusion is reflected in the principle of modern contract law that finds an implied "best efforts" obligation in the acceptance of an exclusive dealership.[4] Without such an obligation, the distributor would have his supplier (or licensor) over a barrel. This would be anticipated, and the supplier, in order to minimize the distributor's power over him, would refuse to consent to a long-term contract. As a result, the length of exclusive contracts would be artificially truncated. (Granted, the contract in *Wood* itself was terminable by either party, without liability, after a year, but a year can be a long time in the fashion business.) The best-efforts obligation in exclusive-dealing arrangements, pioneered in *Wood v. Duff-Gordon*, promotes the achievement of the basic goal of contract law, which is to facilitate the making of long-term commitments. The parties can waive the obligation if they want. But it is the sensible *default rule,* that is, the best approximation to what the parties would have specified had they negotiated over the point.

The imputing of a best-efforts obligation in exclusive-dealing contracts is indeed the cardinal contribution of *Wood* to the law of contracts, and this fact should help us understand Cardozo's distinction as a judge. The issue in the case was the supplier-licensor's (Duff-Gordon's) obligation, not the dealer's (Wood's). The latter was relevant only to supply consideration for the former. Cardozo was able to lay bare the issue that was important to the development of the law, even though that issue was buried in the case. He could not have done this had he said consideration didn't matter; and if he had said this, he would not have carried the court with him. Even if, in the end, law is policy analysis,

4. Uniform Commercial Code, §2-306(2); E. Allan Farnsworth, *Contracts* 530 (1982).

to get the right policy outcome requires distinctively legal techniques, well illustrated by Cardozo's opinions.

Cardozo's project of bringing law into phase with commercial necessity works better in the relatively straightforward cases (as they now appear), such as *Wood v. Duff-Gordon,*[5] than in such baffling cases as *Canadian Industrial Alcohol Co. v. Dunbar Molasses Co.*[6] The defendant had agreed to sell the plaintiff "approximately" 1.5 million gallons of molasses "of the usual run from the National Sugar Refinery, Yonkers, N.Y.," but delivered only 344,083 gallons. When sued, the defendant argued that the duty to deliver was conditional upon the production by the National Sugar Refinery at Yonkers of enough molasses to fill the plaintiff's order. During the period of the contract the refinery produced only 485,848 gallons of molasses—much less than its capacity—and allotted only the 344,083 to the defendant. Cardozo's opinion begins by assuming that, if the refinery had been destroyed, or its output curtailed by the failure of the sugar crop or conceivably by a strike, the contract would indeed have been discharged. But nothing of that sort had been suggested; the opinion does not say *why* the refinery reduced its output, and there is no explanation in the briefs or record. Cardozo is therefore left free to remark without fear of contradiction that "there is nothing to show that the defendant would have been unable by a timely contract with the refinery to have assured itself of a supply sufficient for its needs . . . So far as the record shows, [the defendant] put its faith in the mere chance that the output of the refinery would be the same from year to year . . . The defendant is in no better position than a factor who undertakes in his own name to sell for future delivery a special grade of merchandise to be manufactured by a special mill. The duty will be discharged if the mill is destroyed before delivery is due. The duty will

5. See also Moran v. Standard Oil Co., 211 N.Y. 187, 105 N.E. 217 (1914), and Outlet Embroidery Co. v. Derwent Mills, Ltd., 254 N.Y. 179, 172 N.E. 462 (1930)—other opinions by Cardozo in cases of incomplete contracting.
6. 258 N.Y. 194, 179 N.E. 383 (1932).

subsist if the output is reduced because times turn out to be hard and labor charges high." So the defendant lost.

The last two sentences in the quotation illustrate Cardozo's rhetorical skill. The normal English writer would put a "But" at the beginning of the second sentence or a "however" after "duty" in that sentence. The suppression of the connective not only saves a word but makes the opposition between the two sentences more dramatic, vivid, memorable. Still, it would have been nice if Cardozo had given an *explanation* for the decision. If the defendant had promised to deliver 1.5 million gallons of molasses *simpliciter* and defaulted, he would be limited to such general defenses as the law gives to defaulters, such as the defense of impossibility to which Cardozo alludes. But the contract specified the source of supply, and Cardozo fails to explain the function if any of that specification. If a wholesale grocer promises to supply a restaurant with ten cases of Perrier a week, is he liable for breach of contract if one week the importer tells him that the supply of Perrier is down and he will have to make do with two cases? Is it not more likely that such a contract is implicitly conditioned on availability from the designated source? Bear in mind that my hypothetical contract is not for carbonated mineral water but for *Perrier* carbonated mineral water. There is nothing in Cardozo's opinion, or in the briefs or record, about the practice in the molasses trade, the duties customarily undertaken by middlemen in that trade, and so forth, that would enable these questions to be answered. The plaintiff had argued simply that the contract was unconditional, but this left unclear why the refinery had been mentioned at all. It could, of course, have been mentioned for no particular reason; there frequently is surplusage in contracts, as in statutes and many other types of supposedly carefully drafted document. But Cardozo does not give the reader the materials to enable a choice between the alternative interpretations.

The class of cases just discussed—cases where Cardozo is trying, usually although not always successfully, to make law follow the understanding of the relevant lay community—blends insensibly into a large class of his cases in which he is trying to make law follow the prevalent morality. This, I think, is the light in which we are to understand the famous cases, such as *Allegheny College* and *De Cicco v. Schweizer*,[7] in which Cardozo relaxed the rigors of the consideration doctrine.[8] In all these cases Cardozo seems to be moving toward the goal—which American law still has not reached—of making legally binding, within the institutional limitations of the American judiciary (whose ability to determine the truth in a welter of conflicting allegations is not distinguished), all those promises that the average person in the parties' line of business would think the promisor ought to be legally obligated to perform. Thus Cardozo may, for example, have been impressed by the emphasis laid in the excellent brief for Allegheny College on the irresponsibility of revoking pledges of donations to charities desperately dependent on them, although as noted in chapter 1 it is uncertain whether making those pledges irrevocable will increase or reduce the amount of charitable giving, or leave it unchanged.

The same moralizing tendency is at work in Cardozo's tort opinions, such as *Glanzer v. Shepard*.[9] The plaintiff, Glanzer, had bought from an importer (Bech, Van Siclen & Company) 905 bags of South American beans at an agreed price per pound. The total contract price was specified to be the agreed price per pound times the number of pounds as determined and certified by public weighers. The seller hired the defendants, a firm of public weighers, to weigh the beans and to certify the weight, which they did, sending copies of the certification to both the plaintiff and the seller, as they had been directed to do. The plaintiff took delivery of the beans but when he tried to resell them found they were 11,854 pounds short of the certified weight. He sued the

7. 221 N.Y. 431, 117 N.E. 807 (1917).

8. This is a more realistic way of reading *Allegheny College* than to suppose, as Cardozo claimed, that there actually was a bilateral contract.

9. 233 N.Y. 236, 135 N.E. 275 (1922).

weighers, and Cardozo held for the court that the suit could be maintained. "Assumption of the task of weighing was the assumption of a duty to weigh carefully for the benefit of all whose conduct was to be governed." There was no contract between the plaintiffs and the defendants. But since the latter, "acting, not casually nor as mere servants, but in the pursuit of an independent calling, weighed and certified at the order of one with the very end and aim of shaping the conduct of another," they were liable for their (assumed) carelessness. "Diligence was owing, not only to him who ordered, but to him also who relied."

Glanzer could have sued the seller for breach of contract or unjust enrichment, because the contract surely meant to set a price per actual pound, not a price per pound negligently and inaccurately determined by the public weighers. The opinion does not indicate why he did not follow the obvious route. Nor does the record. The defendants' brief made a point of this, by noting that the trial court had refused to allow them to prove that Bech, Van Siclen & Company was solvent. In effect they challenged Glanzer to explain why he had not sued his seller. Glanzer did not rise to the bait. Maybe some advantageous business relationship between him and the Bech company had made him reluctant to sue the company; but this must remain a conjecture.

The defendants knew that Glanzer would rely on their accurately weighing the beans; and the essential, and one would think readily achievable, undertaking of a public weigher is—to weigh goods accurately. The certificate was thus a guaranty of sorts, although apparently only against a *careless* failure to weigh accurately; there is no suggestion that the weighers would have been strictly liable for the consequences of inaccurate weighing.

A consideration not mentioned by Cardozo strongly supports his result. Although hired by the seller, the weighers were really acting in the interest of the buyer worried that the seller might try to overcharge him by overstating the weight of the goods sold. The buyer wanted an independent third party to determine the weight. The protection given by this measure would be deficient if there were no legal remedy against the weighers' negligence. (Deficient, but not nonexistent, since weighers who develop a reputation for negligence will lose business.) There would be no *effective* legal remedy unless the buyer could sue; the seller is not hurt if the weighers overstate the weight of the shipment.

Cardozo stresses the plaintiff's reliance; "reliance" here is shorthand for the plaintiff's inability to protect himself. Glanzer could have sent his own agent to do the weighing, but the defendants did not suggest that this would have been an efficient method of buyer self-protection. The weighers' care was Glanzer's protection, and the weighers knew that. The consequence of their carelessness was readily foreseeable; in these circumstances the moral sense of the commercial community imposes a duty of care. *Glanzer* is also a case where, as we have seen, the imposition of a duty is necessary to the flexibility, and hence the efficiency, of commercial transacting, since if there is no liability the plaintiff will have to hire his own weigher. Commercial morality is perhaps the same thing as efficiency, and *Glanzer* is an even more persuasive decision when the link is made clear.

The cases discussed thus far support the generalization that Cardozo thought a person should be presumptively liable for the injuries he inflicts if the relevant lay community would think the injurer seriously in the wrong. *Wagner v. International Ry.*[10] is a famous illustration of this master principle. Through the defendant's negligence one of its trains was in a wreck. The plaintiff and his cousin were passengers on the train. The plaintiff joined the search party that was looking for his cousin, and while searching in the dark fell off a trestle and was hurt. He had not been careless, but the question was whether he (unlike a Mrs. Palsgraf) was a foreseeable victim of the railroad's negligence that had caused the train wreck. The court held that he was, because

10. 232 N.Y. 176, 133 N.E. 437 (1921).

"danger invites rescue." This is a fine example of the compressive power of metaphor, reinforced by meter. The two nouns are two-syllable words with the emphasis on the first syllable. The first noun ends with an "r" sound, the second begins with one. This is law as poetry.

One senses in the *Wagner* opinion the further idea that danger *ought* to invite rescue—that it is a moral duty to attempt rescue (perhaps especially in a family case, and remember that the Cardozos were a close-knit family) when the risk to the rescuer is commensurate with the likely benefit to the person sought to be rescued. The opinion could have been strengthened by pointing out that a prudent rescue is desirable even from the railroad's selfish standpoint, since the railroad would be liable to any un-rescued victim of its negligence.[11] Once again the moral and the economic perspectives merge—an important consideration from the standpoint of making a pragmatic jurisprudence more than mere words.

Another case of this type is *Imperator Realty Co. v. Tull*.[12] The defendant orally relaxed a condition in a written contract, and when the plaintiff relied on the oral assurance and omitted the condition, the defendant declared the contract broken. The court held that the defendant was estopped (forbidden) to plead the Statute of Frauds (which makes certain contracts unenforceable unless they are in writing) as a defense to the plaintiff's claim that the contract had been validly, albeit orally, modified. Cardozo concurred, remarking that "we are facing a principle more nearly ultimate than either waiver or estoppel, one with roots in the yet larger principle that no one shall be permitted to found any claim upon his own inequity or take advantage of his own wrong"; and he cited *Riggs v. Palmer*.

Here is an exotic example of the moral concern in Cardozo's

---

11. William M. Landes and Richard A. Posner, *The Economic Structure of Tort Law* 250–251 (1987). Notice the parallel to the suggested analysis of *Riggs v. Palmer* in chapter 2.

12. 228 N.Y. 447, 127 N.E. 263 (1920).

judging. Babington was a taxicab driver employed by the Yellow Taxi Corporation. A policeman jumped on the running board of his taxi and ordered him to chase another car, whose driver the policeman wanted to arrest. Another vehicle cut across Babington's path, causing him to swerve and hit a trolley car. He was injured and eventually died from his injuries. The question was whether his family was entitled to an award of workmen's compensation, and it depended on whether Babington had been in the performance of his duty at the time of the accident. The court, in an opinion by Cardozo, held that he had been.[13] A New York statute made it a misdemeanor to willfully neglect or refuse to aid a policeman in making an arrest. Cardozo purports to trace this statute back to the old English "hue and cry." "The ancient ordinance abides as an interpreter of present duty . . . The incorporeal being, the Yellow Taxi Corporation, would have been bound to respond . . . to the summons of the officer if it had been sitting in the driver's seat. In sending Babington upon the highway, it knew or is chargeable with knowledge that man and car alike would have to answer to the call."

The references to "incorporeal being" and "chargeable with knowledge" are redolent of legal fiction, and as the dissent points out a plausible alternative interpretation to Cardozo's is that when Babington answered the call he became a temporary, ad hoc employee of the New York City police department and ceased to be in the performance of his duties to his permanent employer. The taxi company no longer had a right to direct his performance—a right that, normally, is the sine qua non of the employment relationship and hence of liability to pay workers' compensation. It seems harsh to make the company liable for an injury that may have resulted entirely from the negligence of a public official. It is true that since workers' compensation is a form of strict liability, an employer frequently will be required to compensate a worker injured without fault on the part of the employer or his

13. Babington v. Yellow Taxi Corp., 250 N.Y. 14, 164 N.E. 726 (1928).

other employees. Yet it is hardly to be supposed that, if the government had conscripted Yellow Taxi's drivers, and requisitioned its cabs, for war service (remember the taxis of the Marne), Yellow Taxi would be required to pay compensation to drivers wounded in the fighting. The duty to serve would be the driver's, not his employer's; and maybe the same was true of Babington.

The taxi business is licensed (and was in the 1920s), and maybe part of the consideration for the license is an undertaking to assist the police at the lessee's expense. But the opinions do not explore this angle; nor had the briefs done so. One suspects that Cardozo thought it not very public-spirited of the taxi company to resist the payment of compensation to an employee injured in a higher calling, as it were.

This is a case, and not an isolated one, where the moralistic streak in Cardozo may have led him astray. Not that *Babington* was decided incorrectly; but the analysis is inadequate. The discussion of hue and cry, which occupies the bulk of Cardozo's opinion (needless to say, it had not been mentioned in the briefs) leads nowhere. This becomes apparent when, after stating without explanation that "we have preferred to place the ruling upon the broadest ground available," Cardozo offers a sensible narrow ground: "There is no evidence that the route was any different from the one that would otherwise have been followed, and none that the speed was so changed as to aggravate the danger. Causal connection there was none so far as the record has informed us, between the collision with the trolley car and the presence of the officer on the running board in pursuit of an offender." This is a good ground for decision (and might have been, we recall, in *Hynes* as well); why did Cardozo feel it necessary to reach out for a broader, less tenable ground?

The most famous of Cardozo's moralistic opinions is *Meinhard v. Salmon*.[14] The issue was the duty of a joint venturer toward his coventurer. The court held that it was a fiduciary duty, which

14. 249 N.Y. 458, 164 N.E. 545 (1928).

Cardozo proceeded to define as follows: "A trustee is held to something stricter than the morals of the market place. Not honesty alone, but the punctilio of an honor the most sensitive, is then the standard of behavior." It is possible to object that these are just words, and florid ones at that. But they are memorable words, and they set a tone. They make the difference between an arm's length relationship and a fiduciary relationship vivid, unforgettable. The case is heavily cited (653 times, compared to 827 for *MacPherson,* Cardozo's most influential opinion)—a tribute to the importance of eloquence in law. No judge seems ever to have come up with a better formula with which to express the concept of fiduciary duty. A more informative description of the concept would be that, while normally a party to a contract is entitled, with certain exceptions, to take advantage of the other party's ignorance, a fiduciary is not; he must treat the other party's interests as if they were his own. But this is awfully dry.

Equity cases are rich in examples of a fruitful merger of morality and law. The term "equity" as used by lawyers refers to a body of remedies and principles that supplement and modify strict rules of law in order to make the law more just, more moral; the original equity judges in England were in fact clerics. A number of Cardozo opinions descant with his customary eloquence on the importance of equity and construe the equity powers of the New York courts broadly.[15] But even more interesting are the cases where the spirit of equity is brought into a case at law (that is, a case in which the plaintiff seeks damages rather than an equitable remedy such as an injunction). *Jacob & Youngs, Inc. v. Kent*[16] is illustrative. The plaintiff, a builder, inadvertently

15. For example, Marr v. Tumulty, 256 N.Y. 15, 175 N.E. 356 (1931); Evangelical Lutheran Church v. Sahlem, 254 N.Y. 161, 172 N.E. 455 (1930); Epstein v. Gluckin, 233 N.Y. 490, 135 N.E. 861 (1922); Graf v. Hope Bldg. Corp., 254 N.Y. 1, 171 N.E. 884 (1930) (dissenting opinion). *Meinhard* itself is in this line, since fiduciary duties originated in equity.

16. 230 N.Y. 239, 129 N.E. 889 (1921). Other notable examples are People ex rel. McCanliss v. McCanliss, 255 N.Y. 456, 175 N.E. 129 (1931), and People v. Schmidt, 216 N.Y. 324, 110 N.E. 945 (1915).

failed to install the contractually specified brand of pipe in the house that it built for the defendant. The defendant claimed that he did not have to pay for the house until the plaintiff replaced the pipe, but this would have required extensive demolition, at great expense, and the court held that all the defendant was entitled to was a reduction in the purchase price equal to the reduction in the value of the property—which was slight, and probably zero, since the substitute pipe was of like grade and quality—as a result of the plaintiff's breach. "The willful transgressor must accept the penalty of his transgression. For him there is no occasion to mitigate the rigor of implied conditions. The transgressor whose default is unintentional and trivial may hope for mercy if he will offer atonement for his wrong" (citations omitted). This is not only the language of equity; it is the language of equity when Lord Chancellors (the first equity judges in the Anglo-American legal tradition) were ecclesiastics.

Of further interest in this case is Cardozo's suppression of detail.[17] The contract provided that defective work was to be done over; this cuts against Cardozo's interpretation and is not mentioned, but perhaps the reason is that the substitution was not defective, because the substituted pipe was just as good as the contractually specified pipe, as emphasized in the very fine brief for the contractor. Neither does Cardozo mention that the contract treats the specification of brands as establishing standards, so that the contract specification of "Reading pipe" may simply have meant pipe of equivalent quality to Reading pipe; in that event there was no material breach, although the contract does require the architect's permission for a substitution, and this was not sought. (The contractor argued that the substitution had been completely inadvertent and that was why permission had not been sought.) Evidently Cardozo wanted to make a point about equity and remedies rather than to anatomize the contract.

17. Richard Danzig, *The Capability Problem in Contract Law: Further Readings on Well-Known Cases* 108–128 (1978).

It was a good point, well worth making, and more useful for the guidance of bench and bar than an interpretation of a particular contract. Legal craft values in a traditional sense that emphasizes meticulous accuracy and an unwavering duty to place decision on the narrowest possible ground are here compromised in pursuit of a larger sense of judicial responsibility.

The rhetoric of the opinion is also notable, particularly the opening paragraph:

> The plaintiff built a country residence for the defendant at a cost of upwards of $77,000, and now sues to recover a balance of $3,483.46, remaining unpaid. The work of construction ceased in June, 1914, and the defendant then began to occupy the dwelling. There was no complaint of defective performance until March, 1915. One of the specifications for the plumbing work provides that [quoting the contract].

The use of the term "country residence" and mention of its price (a huge sum in 1914) establish the defendant in the reader's mind as a rich man, who having contentedly occupied the house for almost a year after it was built finds an excuse for withholding the last installment of the purchase price—small change to him but perhaps a large amount to the plaintiff, a firm of contractors. There is no reference to contract or promise even though it is a given that the plaintiff broke the contract. Judge McLaughlin set quite a different tone in his dissent, which begins (after "I dissent"): "The plaintiff did not perform its contract."

Cardozo's project of making law serve human rather than mandarin needs, however worthy a project, often lacks thrust, as we can see in Cardozo's most famous line of opinions—those on scope of liability, running from *MacPherson*[18] to *Ultramares*.[19] (Both *Palsgraf* and *Glanzer* are in this line.) The law in 1916, when *MacPherson* was decided, was that the manufacturer of a

18. MacPherson v. Buick Motor Co., 217 N.Y. 382, 111 N.E. 1050 (1916). For a popular recounting of the case, drawing heavily on the trial record, see David W. Peck, *Decision at Law,* ch. 2 (1961) ("Mr. MacPherson and His Buick").

19. Ultramares Corp. v. Touche, 255 N.Y. 170, 174 N.E. 441 (1931).

defective product that injured a consumer was not liable for negligence unless the manufacturer had a contract with the consumer. There was an exception for abnormally dangerous products, however, and it was broadly construed in New York, which gave Cardozo the leverage necessary to persuade a majority of his colleagues—in an opinion fairly describable as a *tour de force* of judicial casuistry[20]—that the exception had swallowed the rule.[21] MacPherson had bought from an auto dealer an automobile manufactured by Buick that had a defective wheel which disintegrated while MacPherson was driving. He was seriously injured and sued Buick. Buick had bought the wheel from another manufacturer and had failed to notice the defect, which a reasonable inspection would have revealed. Buick had not inspected the wheels at all, although it did test drive every car before delivery to the dealer.

Most of Cardozo's opinion is devoted to analysis of precedents, and only once does he turn practical: "The dealer was indeed the one person of whom it might be said with some approach to certainty that by him the car would not be used. Yet the defendant would have us say that he was the one person whom it was under a legal duty to protect." This is not so weird as Cardozo makes it sound. The dealer warrants the safety of the automobile to the consumer but cannot warrant its safety to himself. The injured consumer can sue the dealer under the warranty; the dealer in turn can try to shift the ultimate burden of liability to the manufacturer through the doctrine of indemnity or through an express contract; and the manufacturer can try to shift the liability to the maker of the defective part, also through either the doctrine of indemnity or an express contract. The pragmatic issue in *MacPherson,* which Cardozo does not discuss, is whether the allocation of liability for product injuries should be left to

20. The classic discussion is Edward H. Levi, *An Introduction to Legal Reasoning* 9–25 (1949).

21. *Prosser and Keeton on the Law of Torts* 682–683 (5th ed., W. Page Keeton gen'l ed., 1984).

contract (or to the doctrine, loosely contractual, of implied indemnity) or made a task for tort law. There are practical reasons for the second choice—for example, the possibility that the dealer will lack sufficient assets to pay a judgment and will therefore not be fully deterrable by a suit for damages, and the desirability of avoiding circuitous litigation (consumer versus dealer, followed by dealer versus manufacturer, rather than consumer versus manufacturer). But the opinion does not mention these reasons, although they had been emphasized in the excellent brief filed on MacPherson's behalf by attorney Edgar T. Brackett.

*MacPherson* is Cardozo's most important opinion in terms of impact on the law. Carefully qualified though it was, modest though it was in pretending to be restating rather than changing the law of New York, reticent as it was about the policy considerations relevant to the change it made, the opinion nevertheless managed to change profoundly the climate of opinion regarding privity of contract.[22] Yet on reflection it should be apparent that it is the very caution, modesty, and reticence of the opinion that explain its rapid adoption by other states. *MacPherson* is the quietest of revolutionary manifestos, the least unsettling to conservative professional sensibilities. Cardozo carefully avoids sounding the passionate, populist note of Brackett's brief. There is no better illustration of Cardozo's rhetorical tact.

But *MacPherson* and *Glanzer* make Cardozo's subsequent decisions in *H.R. Moch Co. v. Rensselaer Water Co.*[23] and in *Ultramares* puzzling. The defendant in *Moch* had agreed to supply the City of Rensselaer with water of specified pressure for the city's mains. A fire broke out in a building adjoining the plaintiff's warehouse. The water company was notified of the fire but failed to keep up

22. Id. at 683; Fowler V. Harper, Fleming James, Jr., and Oscar S. Gray, *The Law of Torts*, vol. 4, §25.18B, at p. 629 n. 3 (1986); Warren A. Seavey, "The Waterworks Cases and Stare Decisis," 66 *Harvard Law Review* 84, 86 (1952); Judith S. Kaye, "The Human Dimension in Appellate Judging: A Brief Reflection on a Timeless Concern," 73 *Cornell Law Review* 1004, 1012 (1988).

23. 247 N.Y. 160, 159 N.E. 896 (1928).

the pressure. As a result, the fire department could not extinguish the fire and the warehouse was destroyed. Cardozo opines that even if the failure of pressure was due to negligence on the defendant's part, the plaintiff could not obtain damages. Yet the consequences of inadequate water pressure were foreseeable—this was not a *Palsgraf* type of case—and the fact that the plaintiff was not a party to the city's contract with the defendant should not have mattered after *Glanzer* and *MacPherson*. Cardozo treated it as a case in which the plaintiff was seeking damages for a pure failure by the defendant to rescue his property from a fire for which the defendant bore no responsibility. That is equivalent to excusing medical malpractice on the ground that the doctor did not make the patient ill in the first place.

Cardozo's underlying concern in *Moch* appears to have been with the potential extent of liability, a consideration stressed in the water company's brief. The same concern is evident in *Ultramares*, a decision that has not stood the test of time.[24] The plaintiff incurred losses in making loans in reliance on an audit of the borrower's books. Much as in *Glanzer*, the loan agreement required the borrower to hire public accountants to certify his financial soundness. They conducted an audit and did so negligently. The legal issue was whether they owed a duty of care to persons who transacted with the firm they had audited and who did so in reliance on the audit. So far, the case seems just like *Glanzer*, which Cardozo feebly distinguishes on the ground that the audit was "only incidentally or collaterally for the use of those to whom [the borrower] might exhibit it thereafter." The real difference between the cases is the greater potential extent of liability in *Ultramares*, a point stressed both in Touche's brief and in an amicus curiae brief of the American Institute of Accountants, much as it had been stressed by the water company in *Moch*.

---

24. Although it has its defenders. For a full discussion, see John A. Siliciano, "Negligent Accounting and the Limits of Instrumental Tort Reform," 86 *Michigan Law Review* 1929 (1988).

Cardozo made the point the pivot of the decision, stating: "If liability for negligence exists, a thoughtless slip or blunder, the failure to detect a theft or forgery beneath the cover of deceptive entries, may expose accountants to a liability in an indeterminate amount for an indeterminate time to an indeterminate class. The hazards of a business conducted on these terms are so extreme as to enkindle doubt whether a flaw may not exist in the implication of a duty that exposes to these consequences."

This is wonderfully stated—just how wonderfully is best seen from a comparison with what must have been its source, a passage in the brief of the American Institute of Accountants: "To hold professional men, and those conducting a business which in its nature is similar to professional work, liable to persons other than those, either to whom they have rendered a service or with whom they have come into direct relationship, jointly liable to an unlimited number of persons in an unlimited amount, and perhaps for an unlimited time, would, it is respectfully submitted, be neither equitable nor expedient" (p. 61). By rearranging and tightening up the passage and changing "unlimited" to the more accurate and impressive "indeterminate," Cardozo turns dross into gold.

Here may be a good place to consider the general question of the "value added" by Cardozo's opinions to the lawyers' briefs. Judges' opinions do not acknowledge the borrowing of ideas, even language, from the parties' briefs, so the evaluation of a judge's creativity requires comparison between the opinion and the briefs in each case. I have done this for the cases discussed in this book that Cardozo wrote on the New York Court of Appeals. The briefs turn out to be for the most part competent and well written, as well as temperate and civil (with occasional exceptions, one mentioned in the next chapter). They are, I am distressed to say, superior on average to the briefs I have been reading for the last eight years as a federal appellate judge. But they bear slight resemblance to Cardozo's opinions. Not only in style, but in the order of issues and in the facts and arguments emphasized, his opinions owe little even to those briefs that are excellent. The example I gave of his paraphrasing a passage from a brief appears to be unusual in Cardozo's opinions—and yet it shows a master's touch as unmistakably as Shakespeare's paraphrases of Sir Thomas North's translations of Plutarch.[25]

To return to the issues in *Ultramares,* the passage concerning indeterminacy of liability would have fit *MacPherson* or any other products liability case involving a mass-produced good. Accountants know that their audits are relied on by investors and others who deal with the audited firm, and they can buy liability insurance to protect themselves from crushing liability for negligence. The principle of *Ultramares* has been rejected in most states, yet the sky has not fallen on the accounting profession. While it is true that even without the threat of legal liability hanging over their heads accountants will have market incentives to maintain a reputation for care (and if a firm of accountants is about to go out of business and therefore doesn't care about its reputation, there is a fair likelihood that it does not have enough assets to make a lawsuit against it worthwhile either), automobile manufacturers have market incentives to make safe cars. So again it is not obvious how *MacPherson* can be distinguished.

Remarking in conclusion in *Ultramares* that "our holding does not emancipate accountants from the consequences of fraud," Cardozo expresses "doubt whether the average business man receiving a certificate without paying for it and receiving it merely as one among a multitude of possible investors, would look for anything more." This is an attempt to dissolve the legal question into one of commercial practice. But take away the "multitude" and it is *Glanzer* exactly; with the multitude, it is *MacPherson.* Cardozo is unable to explain why the greater the potential harm from a defendant's negligence, the more circumscribed liability should be.

25. Of which I give an example in *Law and Literature: A Misunderstood Relation* 346–347 (1988).

That Cardozo's opinions in *MacPherson* and *Glanzer* do not hang together with those in *Moch* and *Ultramares* may seem a serious defect in Cardozo's judicial performance; I think it is. Yet it has served rather to magnify than to diminish his reputation, thus illustrating the normative ambiguity of the concept. The line of opinions I have been discussing demonstrates the importance of generality, of omnisignificance—of "something for everyone"—to reputation. Cardozo wrote opinions that can be invoked by judges and scholars who want to broaden the scope of liability, and also opinions that can be invoked by judges and scholars who want to limit or reduce that scope. Such were his narrative and casuistical skills that each set of opinions is a powerful support for one of the opposing positions, while the apparent (and I think real) inconsistency between the two sets provides a challenge to the imaginative powers of law professors, students, trial lawyers, and judges.

Moreover, on the score of consistency it is important to distinguish between results and rationales. There are factual differences between *Ultramares* and *Moch* on one hand and *Glanzer* and *MacPherson* on the other that might make all four decisions correct. The extent of potential liability was more difficult to predict in the first pair of cases than in the second pair, and such difficulty in turn makes it difficult for a defendant to know how much care is optimal to take. It is true that as a matter of abstract principle once we have decided that a defendant is negligent we have decided that he should have known to take more care. But in many tort cases, including both *Ultramares* and *Moch,* the defendant is liable only by virtue of the doctrine of *respondeat superior,* a doctrine of strict liability: the defendant is liable because its employee was negligent. No large enterprise can prevent every one of its employees from ever committing a negligent act, so the enterprise must decide how many resources to devote to selection and supervision of employees. It cannot make a rational decision if it cannot ascertain the costs it will incur if it fails to prevent negligence by its employees.

In both types of case, moreover, if there was an actionable tort, there was quite likely to be a multitude of victims; and methods for handling the "mass tort" were far less developed in the 1920s than they are today. Even today, the sheer unwieldiness of such litigation has persuaded many thoughtful observers that alternative methods of regulation must be found to that of the common law. Also, in both cases, the potential victims of the defendant's negligence had methods of self-protection. An investor (including a lender, the plaintiff in *Ultramares*) can diversify his portfolio of investments (or loans) to reduce—possibly to eliminate—any impact from a fall in the value of one of them. He can also rely on additional sources of information besides an accountant's audit. Property owners can take steps to reduce the danger of fire and can buy fire insurance.[26]

The points are related. They suggest—no stronger word is possible—that the victims in these two cases may have been superior loss avoiders to the injurers. My own view is that *Moch* is correct but *Ultramares* incorrect. The city was acting as the agent of its residents in negotiating with the water company, and the water company was entitled to assume that if it was to be the fire insurer for the city's property the city would compensate it accordingly. The water company's brief argued that the company's remuneration ($42.50 per year per hydrant, of which there were 197, making a total price of $8,372.50) was too slight to warrant an inference that the company had undertaken to insure the property owners of Rensselaer against the potentially catastrophic consequences of a negligent failure to maintain the pressure in the mains. The company added the further, ingenious

26. Charles O. Gregory, "Gratuitous Undertakings and the Duty of Care," 1 *De Paul Law Review* 30, 59–60 (1951). Notice incidentally that the purchase of insurance and the diversification of a portfolio are analytically similar—they spread rather than prevent losses. But spreading, like preventing, is a way of reducing the disutility, and hence cost, of an injury. Richard A. Posner and Andrew M. Rosenfield, "Impossibility and Related Doctrines in Contract Law: An Economic Analysis," 6 *Journal of Legal Studies* 83 (1977).

argument that since the nonliability of water companies for property damage resulting from failure to maintain pressure was well settled at the time its contract with the city was written, the absence of a special provision imposing liability shows that no such liability was contemplated. Of course, the plaintiff was not a party to the contract, but it would be rather one-sided to stick the company with liability when it had no reasonable opportunity to negotiate for compensation for bearing that liability. The plaintiff did not attempt to rebut these arguments.

Touche argued similarly in the suit against it that the fee for the audit (a measly $1,138) was incommensurate with the claims arising from the negligent performance of the audit ($683,000). The difference is that, while the investor may well look to the accountant as a guarantor of the corporation's financial representations, the property owner does not look to the water company as its fire insurer. But the important point is that there are enough arguably relevant factual differences among the scope-of-liability cases to make the inconsistencies in Cardozo's analysis of them a challenge rather than an intellectual disgrace.

In a case on scope of liability that I have not yet discussed Cardozo does make some practical arguments for limiting liability. *Kerr S.S. Co. v. Radio Corp. of America*[27] involved the liability of a telegraph company for consequential damages (essentially lost profits) resulting from the company's failure to transmit the plaintiff's telegram. The failure caused the plaintiff to lose a valuable contract. The suit was in tort, for breach of a public service corporation's duty, but the court held that the rule of *Hadley v. Baxendale*—the famous English case that limits consequential damages in contract suits to those that are foreseeable—applied. In defense of this result Cardozo explained, more fully than in any of his other cases, the reasons for limiting the scope of liability:

27. 245 N.Y. 284, 157 N.E. 140 (1927).

Much may be said in favor of the social policy of a rule whereby the companies have been relieved of liabilities that might otherwise be crushing. The sender can protect himself by insurance in one form or another if the risk of nondelivery or error appears to be too great. The total burden is not heavy since it is distributed among many, and can be proportioned in any instance to the loss likely to ensue. The company, if it takes out insurance for itself, can do no more than guess at the loss to be avoided. To pay for this unknown risk, it will be driven to increase the rates payable by all, though the increase is likely to result in the protection of a few.

This does not exhaust the relevant considerations, although it is a good start. Cardozo could in addition have noted a point stressed by the telegraph company, that it offered for a 25 percent premium a repeated-message service (that is, transmission twice rather than just once). If the steamship company had been that concerned with the prompt transmission of its cable, it should have bought that service.

The record in *Kerr* shows that the telegraph company had a copy of the same codebook the steamship company had used to encode its message.[28] Yet Cardozo's opinion states that while the telegraph company "upon receiving from a steamship company a long telegram in cipher to be transmitted to Manila would naturally infer that the message had relation to business of some sort," "beyond that, it could infer nothing." This is an inaccuracy but not a material one. The record in *Kerr* reveals that the codebook in the telegraph company's office was for the convenience of customers who might want to code or decode messages on the spot. The telegraph company did not decode the messages it was asked to transmit; nor would its customers have wanted it to do so; and doing so would have delayed transmission.

As illustrated by his failure to mention the repeated-message service, Cardozo did not always exploit the facts of his cases to the full. Nor did he explore pertinent policy considerations as probingly, as tenaciously, as he might have done. But fact and

28. This is stressed in E. Allan Farnsworth, "Legal Remedies for Breach of Contract," 70 *Columbia Law Review* 1145, 1207 n. 261 (1970).

policy are opaque and elusive without a framework, and what Cardozo principally lacked in wrestling with cases in which intuitions of substantive justice ran out was an incisive framework for, or technique of, policy analysis such as modern economic analysis provides. He can hardly be blamed for failing to use tools developed long after his death, however, and we can find intimations of the economic approach, notably in *Adams v. Bullock*.[29] The defendant operated a trolley line powered by uninsulated overhead wires, as in *Hynes*. The line ran under a bridge used by pedestrians. The plaintiff, a boy of twelve, strolled across the bridge swinging a wire eight feet long. One of the swings carried the wire over the wall of the bridge, and it touched the overhead wires, causing an electrical shock that injured the boy seriously. Cardozo's court threw out a verdict for him. The opinion notes that, since uninsulated electric wires are highly dangerous, the defendant was required to exercise a high degree of care. But since the wires in question were so placed that no one using the bridge could reach them even by bending over the parapet that ran along the side of the bridge—the wires were more than four and a half feet below the top of the parapet—the danger to people on the bridge was slight. This did not end the analysis. "Chance of harm, though remote, may betoken negligence, if needless. Facility of protection may impose a duty to protect." This anticipates the Hand formula ($B < PL$, where $B$ is the burden of precautions that would avoid the accident, $P$ is the probability of the accident, and $L$ is the magnitude of the harm if the accident occurs) and the cost-benefit analysis of negligence that has been built on it.[30] (More precisely, the *Adams* opinion and the Hand formula elaborate on the longstanding approach, inarticulately economic, used by common law judges to decide negligence cases.) Even if $PL$ is low because $P$ is low ("chance of

29. 227 N.Y. 208, 125 N.E. 93 (1919).

30. Landes and Posner, note 11 above, at 97–98, 102. The Hand formula is from Judge Learned Hand's opinion in United States v. Carroll Towing Co., 159 F.2d 169 (2d Cir. 1947).

harm . . . remote"), the defendant may be negligent because *B* is *very* low (protection is easy). However, "there is . . . a distinction, not to be ignored, between electric light and trolley wires. The distinction is that the former may be insulated"; it is in this connection that Cardozo makes the remark about a needless chance of harm, and about facility of protection, that I quoted above. With trolley wires, "insulation is impossible. Guards here and there are of little value. To avert the possibility of this accident and others like it at one point or another on the route, the defendant must have abandoned the overhead system, and put the wires underground . . . To hold it liable upon the facts exhibited in this record would be to charge it as an insurer." Except for the point about insulation not being feasible for trolley wires, Cardozo's proto-economic analysis owes nothing to the briefs.

I will not bore the reader with endless case analyses, but I cannot resist exhibiting a few more of the epigrammatic utterances that, together with the remarkable fact statements, are the source of Cardozo's particular and abiding charm as a judicial writer. "The soundness of a conclusion may not infrequently be tested by its consequences."[31] (Pragmatism in a nutshell.) "Jurisdiction exists that rights may be maintained. Rights are not maintained that jurisdiction may exist."[32] "The reverberating clang of those accusatory words would drown all weaker sounds. It is for ordinary minds, and not for psychoanalysts, that our rules of evidence are framed. They have their source very often in considerations of administrative convenience, of practical expediency, and not in rules of logic. When the risk of confusion is so great as to upset the balance of advantage, the evidence goes out."[33] "A system of procedure is perverted from its proper function when it multiplies impediments to justice without the war-

31. Ostrowe v. Lee, 256 N.Y. 36, 175 N.E. 505 (1931).
32. Berkovitz v. Arbib & Houlberg, Inc., 230 N.Y. 261, 130 N.E. 288 (1921).
33. Shepard v. United States, 290 U.S. 96, 104 (1933).

rant of clear necessity."[34] "Metaphors in law are to be narrowly watched, for starting as devices to liberate thought, they end often by enslaving it."[35]

Although Cardozo's judicial prose is occasionally plummy, there are many more analytic than stylistic flaws in his opinions. The characteristic analytic flaw, of which I have presented several examples already, is the substitution of words for thought. My last quotation was from *Berkey v. Third Avenue Ry.,* a case in which a woman injured as the result of a motorman's negligence as she was getting off a streetcar sued not the streetcar company (a corporation) but instead the corporation that owned it. Ordinarily a shareholder, even a corporate one, is not liable for the debts (tort or contract) of the corporation in which it owns shares; and Cardozo refused to let Berkey "pierce the corporate veil" of the motorman's employer and sue the employer's owner. Why she wanted to do so is completely unclear from the opinion. Cardozo states that the subsidiary was fully solvent, and this eliminates one obvious motive, but no other is offered. However, in his opening statement to the jury, Berkey's lawyer had argued that, when he filed his complaint against the parent corporation two months before the statute of limitations expired, he had not known of the existence of the subsidiary. The parent had asked for an extension of time within which to file its answer, to make sure (according to Berkey's lawyer anyway) that the answer— pleading the defense of limited liability—would be filed after the statute of limitations for suing the subsidiary had run. There is no mention of any of this in Cardozo's opinion.

Why in the circumstances disclosed by the trial record Cardozo refused to let Berkey pierce the corporate veil is unclear. He says that the whole subject of parent-subsidiary relations "is still enveloped in the mists of metaphor," but he makes no effort to

34. Reed v. Allen, 286 U.S. 191, 209 (1932) (dissenting opinion).
35. Berkey v. Third Avenue Ry., 244 N.Y. 84, 155 N.E. 58 (1926).

dispel them. "Dominion may be so complete, interference so ob-
trusive, that by the general rules of agency the parent will be a
principal and the subsidiary an agent. Where control is less than
this, we are remitted to the tests of honesty and justice." These
are not tests, and Cardozo is no more able to explain why they
should prevent piercing the corporate veil than he was able to
explain why considerations of justice and policy justified a judgment for Hynes's estate.

In *Cullings v. Goetz,*[36] the question was whether a landlord's
breach of his covenant (promise) to repair a garage he had leased
made him liable in tort to a guest of the lessee, injured entering
the garage when the garage door fell on him. The door was
known to be unsafe, and the owner had promised the lessee to
repair it. Cardozo declared for a unanimous court that there was
no liability. The only reason he gave for this conclusion—so
patently in tension with *MacPherson,* which he did not cite—is
that the rule of nonliability to a third party for breach of the
landlord's covenant to repair, whether "wise or unwise in its
origin, has worked itself by common acquiescence into the tissues
of our law. It is too deeply imbedded to be superseded or ignored.
Hardly a day goes by in our great centers of population
but it is applied by judges and juries in cases great and small."
So what? Cardozo's rather corny remarks do not distinguish the
rule from any of the other vestigial anachronisms with which
the common law of land occupiers' liability is encumbered. As
Cardozo notes in the opinion, there were contrary dicta in a number of New York cases, several states had rejected the rule, and
the American Law Institute in its restatement of torts had come
out against it. Why was it not ripe for reexamination? Cardozo
does not say, but my guess is that he did not think he could carry
a majority of his colleagues with him and saw no point in dissenting. Every dissent is an irritant to the members of the
majority; hence a judge who dissents at the drop of a hat jeopar-

36. 256 N.Y. 287, 176 N.E. 397 (1931).

dizes the esteem of his colleagues. Moreover, by presenting himself as out of step with the rest of the court, the chronic dissenter makes it less likely that they will look to him for leadership. Gadflies are not leaders, though they may become leaders (the case of Black and Rehnquist), and even if they never become institutional leaders may exert great influence on thought in the long run. Cardozo wanted to be an institutional leader and succeeded in this aim, in part by avoiding the pose of an ostentatious liberal.[37] It took forty-five years for the New York Court of Appeals to get around to overruling *Cullings* as being out of step with modern thinking about landlords' liability.[38]

I have said nothing about Cardozo's contribution to the jurisprudence of the Supreme Court, on which he served for the last quarter of his judicial career—with great distinction, if one can judge from the citation history of his opinions (see chapter 5). Whether because Cardozo was the junior member of a court in which cases were not assigned by rotation, or because Chief Justice Hughes hogged a disproportionate number of the best cases for himself, or because Cardozo was frequently in dissent, or because the work or working conditions of the Supreme Court did not suit his temperament, or because many of the issues that preoccupied the Court in the 1930s have proved transitory (but torts and contracts are eternal), or because six years is too short a time for a Supreme Court justice to make his mark (given the exceptional breadth of the Court's jurisdiction and the relatively small number of majority opinions that each justice writes)—and Cardozo did not have a full six years of actual service on the Court, because of his terminal illness—Cardozo did not place a strongly individual imprint on any field of Supreme Court

37. And so we find cases such as Dougherty v. Salt, 227 N.Y. 200, 125 N.E. 94 (1919), where Cardozo refused to enforce a contract on the ground that there was no consideration, and Sun Printing & Publishing Ass'n v. Remington Paper & Power Co., 235 N.Y. 338, 139 N.E. 470 (1923), where, over a powerful dissent by Crane, he denied enforcement of a contract on the ground of indefiniteness.

38. Putnam v. Stout, 38 N.Y.2d 607, 345 N.E.2d 319 (1976).

jurisprudence. (Figure 6 in chapter 5 supports this impression.) Cardozo's opinions, both majority and separate, are above the average for Supreme Court opinions, then or now, but they lack the verve and punch of his opinions for the New York Court of Appeals, and a sense of constraint is palpable. His few landmark opinions are mainly of historical interest, such as the opinions upholding the constitutionality of the social security statute.[39] But his proposal in *Palko v. Connecticut*[40] to make the concept of "ordered liberty" the standard for deciding which protections of the Bill of Rights to apply to the states through the due process clause of the Fourteenth Amendment, although rejected by the modern Court, is of enduring interest—and may be on the rebound.[41] And his concurring opinion in *Schechter* and his dissent in *Carter Coal* make a powerful case for applying a rule of reason approach to the scope of Congress's power to regulate economic activities that affect interstate or foreign commerce.[42] Every economic activity, however local, affects interstate commerce because of the chain of substitutions that connects all activities in a national economy. But Cardozo recognized that to infer from this that Congress could regulate all local activity would wreck the balance between state and federal regulatory power that the Constitution had struck in empowering Congress to regulate interstate and foreign—not all—commerce. He thought a line should be drawn that would, however crudely, balance the competing values of nationalism and localism. Perhaps his approach will someday persuade a majority of justices.

Many of Cardozo's Supreme Court opinions, however, reflect

---

39. Steward Machine Co. v. Davis, 301 U.S. 548 (1937); Helvering v. Davis, 301 U.S. 619 (1937).

40. 302 U.S. 319 (1937).

41. Teague v. Lane, 109 S. Ct. 1060, 1073 (1989).

42. A.L.A. Schechter Poultry Corp. v. United States, 295 U.S. 495, 554 (1935); Carter v. Carter Coal Co., 298 U.S. 238, 327–328 (1936).

an uncritical acceptance of rationales for New Deal legislation that seem to a modern understanding naive. And two of his most heavily cited opinions—*Gully v. First National Bank*[43] and *United States v. Swift & Co.*[44]—are, although not political, highly controversial. *Gully* attempted, without great success,[45] to define the circumstances in which a claim may be said to "arise under" federal law, thereby conferring jurisdiction on the federal courts to enforce the claim. *Swift* places an exceedingly—probably excessively—heavy burden on a party seeking to modify a consent decree that may have been entered many years earlier and in radically different circumstances. Later cases have modified the burden significantly.[46]

A career is to a significant extent a matter of luck; and it may be that Cardozo's luck deserted him when he was appointed to the Supreme Court. Although the appointment may have conferred a slight halo effect, six more years on the New York Court of Appeals might have raised Cardozo's reputation to an even higher level than it has attained—and as with Learned Hand and Henry Friendly, people would be saying what a shame it was that Cardozo was never appointed to the Supreme Court and what a super job he would have done if he had been. He did well on the Court, but his performance was an anticlimax.

The times may have been at fault, not Cardozo. The 1930s may just have been a trough in judicial creativity, a time when the initiative for reform, at both the state and federal levels, shifted for a time to nonjudicial reformers such as the members of the American Law Institute (of course Cardozo was one) and the drafters of the Federal Rules of Civil Procedure. The judicial

43. 299 U.S. 109 (1936).
44. 286 U.S. 106 (1932).
45. *Hart and Wechsler's The Federal Courts and the Federal System* 998–999 (Paul M. Bator et al., eds., 3d ed. 1988).
46. For example, see New York State Association for Retarded Children v. Carey, 706 F.2d 956, 967–970 (2d Cir. 1983) (Friendly, J.).

wave was to crest again in the 1940s. It is impossible to know whether Cardozo, had he lived, would have risen to the challenge. But one may venture the suggestion that, as Fortinbras said of Hamlet, "he was likely, had he been put on, / To have prov'd most royal."

# 7

# A Summary with Comparisons

IT DOES NOT REQUIRE even a short book to establish that Cardozo is a famous judge. But the evidence presented in chapter 5 goes some way toward showing that his fame is anchored in a solidly *professional* reputation. His opinions are more heavily cited than those of the judges, including the most distinguished judges, he served with. This is true not only of his service on the New York Court of Appeals but, surprisingly, of his service on the Supreme Court as well, after correction is made for the fact that he was out of step with the majority of his colleagues on the Supreme Court. More than half a century after his resignation from the New York Court of Appeals, opinions that Cardozo wrote for that court remain a staple of legal education and a focus of legal scholarship. It appears that in the opinion of the legal profession, Cardozo is the outstanding American common law judge—alternatively, though not quite equivalently, the outstanding state judge—of the twentieth century.

Which is not to say that he is the most influential. Fame and influence must be distinguished. Cardozo's influence even on the fields of his greatest eminence—torts and contracts—was limited. If we ask whether today's law of torts and contract would be different if Cardozo had never lived, the answer is probably not. The question may seem unfair; we might get the same answer to the question whether physics would be different today if Cardozo's approximate contemporary Einstein had never lived. If you remove one person from history, you make room for others to make his discoveries, his contributions; they may take longer to make, but eventually the field catches up and after a long enough time the effect of any given individual will have dissipated completely. But even if we ask a more confined question about influence—did Cardozo change the law of his time, which is to say, make it change sooner than it would have had he not lived?—the answer is uncertain. The vast majority of his opinions apply established principles without altering them. *MacPherson* is a notable exception; also the opinions such as *Wood v. Duff-Gordon* on implied obligations, and perhaps *Palko* on "ordered liberty." These and a few others are *generative* opinions, but the total number is small.

Cardozo was an incrementalist working primarily in an incremental medium, the common law; we do not expect or find in his work seismic changes in existing law. We do find considerable clarification and highlighting of principles, rationalizing of results, general tidying of legal doctrine: arts of exposition and synthesis rather than of intellectual creativity. The primary impact of Cardozo's work, both judicial and nonjudicial, may well have been pedagogical in the best sense, and is reflected in his deserved popularity among authors of legal teaching materials. He made law clearer, more interesting, more intelligible. As far as changing the law is concerned, he nudged the law a little closer to the pragmatic goal of making law a fully effective, fully rational instrument of social welfare; yet, consistent with his essential moderateness, only a little.

Influential or not, Cardozo certainly was and is eminent, and I want now, recapitulating and extending the discussion in earlier chapters, to explain his eminence. Probably the most important factor is the *rhetoric* of Cardozo's opinions. I include in this term not only his writing style narrowly conceived but also the architecture of his opinions. The best of them are memorable for the drama and clarity of their statements of fact, the brevity and verve of their legal discussion, the sparkle of their epigrams, the air of culture, the panache with which precedents are marshaled and dispatched, the idiosyncratic but effective departures from standard English prose style. The opinions have a charm that is literary, essayistic—at times theatrical and even musical. The charm owes nothing to the briefs; it is the product of Cardozo's own literary skill.

The second most important factor in Cardozo's eminence may well be his judicial program, clearly stated in *The Nature of the Judicial Process,* of bringing law closer to the (informed) nonlawyer's sense of justice. It is often thought a dreadful thing for a judge to have an "agenda"; the judge is supposed to be a tabula rasa, calling the shots as he sees them. The best judges, however, recognizing both the inherent and the contingent shortcomings of the legislative process, have wanted to change the law and have succeeded in doing so. Cardozo wanted to scrape off the barnacles with which law was (and still is) encrusted, and in particular he wanted to discard artificial barriers to liability such as the requirement of privity of contract in products liability cases and the rigid insistence that a promise to be legally enforceable be supported by consideration. *Defore* can be understood in this light; to a nonlawyer, the exclusionary rule is an artificial barrier to convicting criminals.[1] Cardozo wanted law to be shaped by social need rather than by the formal values internal to the legal enterprise, such as conceptual tidiness and consistency with precedent. He got some help here from the lawyers' briefs, but not much.

An important part of Cardozo's rhetorical skill was his ability

---

1. This attitude emerges more clearly in another search and seizure case, where Cardozo, presciently, holds that evidence, and not just contraband or fruits of crime, seized in a lawful search may be retained for use against the defendant at his trial. *People v. Chiagles,* 237 N.Y. 193, 142 N.E. 583 (1923). "We are not to strain an immunity to the point at which human nature rebels against honoring it in conduct. The peace officer empowered to arrest must be empowered to disarm. If he may disarm, he may search, lest a weapon be concealed. The search being lawful, he retains what he finds if connected with the crime. We may be sure that the law would be flouted and derided if, defeating its own ends, it drew too fine a point, after sanctioning the search, between the things to be retained and the things to be returned."

to sugarcoat the pragmatist pill (most strikingly in *MacPherson*) so that not only his judicial colleagues but the entire legal establishment accepted him as a consummate insider rather than fearing him as a bomb-throwing radical. This accomplishment—remarkable in a Jew in the era in which Cardozo lived, but putting one in mind of Disraeli[2] and of the anti-Semitic crack that "Jews are just like other people, only more so"—is due partly to the civility and moderation of the Cardozo persona but mainly to the respect with which Cardozo treated, or in some cases pretended to treat, precedent. He accomplished the remarkable feat of being innovative and antiformalist without being controversial. It is possible that other great judges such as Holmes and Brandeis would have gotten their way more often than they did if they had imitated Cardozo's rhetorical *subtlety*.

Other factors contributing to Cardozo's professional eminence are:

1. His appointment to the Supreme Court, especially as Holmes's anointed successor, enhanced Cardozo's fame and may have cast a retrospective glow over his state court opinions. But I doubt that the effect was great. The appointment was noteworthy mainly because Cardozo had already achieved such professional eminence; it was one of the few times in our history that the most qualified candidate to fill a vacancy on the Supreme Court was the one actually picked for the vacancy. In chapter 5 we saw that Cardozo's state court opinions were not cited appreciably more frequently (relative to contemporaneous opinions by his colleagues) after he was appointed to the Supreme Court than they had been before; the halo effect was small. If we think of the other judges who have been appointed to the Supreme Court after substantial judicial experience, ranging from Holmes to Burger, it is difficult to find any tendency toward upward revaluation of

---

2. Another possible link between Cardozo and Disraeli is that both had a touch of the exotic about them; I noted in chapter 3 the exotic character of Cardozo's writing style.

the appointee's previous judicial accomplishments. If anything, Holmes's notable service on the Supreme Court has distracted scholars from close study of his opinions on the Masssachusetts court.

2. The New York Court of Appeals was the nation's premier commercial court from long before Cardozo was appointed till after he left,[3] in part because of New York's commercial preeminence, in part because federal law was less pervasive than it has since become, in part because the making of commercial law had been left largely to judges rather than being taken over by the legislature. His court's preeminence may well have been a factor in Cardozo's having such rich opportunities for contributing to contract law, but one might suppose that his even greater distinction in tort law could not be explained on this ground; accident cases arose everywhere there were railroads, streetcars, and automobiles. *Glanzer,* however, one of Cardozo's most famous tort cases, arose in a commercial setting, as did *Kerr*. And as the economically most advanced state in the nation, New York had more automobiles[4] (*MacPherson*), and no doubt more railroad traffic (*Wagner, Palsgraf, Hynes*) and trolley traffic (*Adams*), than any other state. This may have contributed to the unusual number of interesting tort cases that came before the court of appeals.

3. Cardozo's extralegal writings, in particular *The Nature of the Judicial Process,* enhanced his standing in the legal profession and

---

3. Some evidence for this proposition is found in a study of citations in a sample of state supreme courts not including the New York Court of Appeals. For a period long predating Cardozo's tenure on that court, the courts in the sample cited New York cases more frequently than those of any other state other than that of the citing court. Lawrence M. Friedman, Robert A. Kagan, Bliss Cartwright, and Stanton Wheeler, "State Supreme Courts: A Century of Style and Citation," 33 *Stanford Law Review* 773, 805–806 (1981). For similar findings, but relating to a later period, see John Henry Merryman, "Toward a Theory of Citations: An Empirical Study of the Citation Practice of the California Supreme Court in 1950, 1960, and 1970," 50 *Southern California Law Review* 381, 402 (1977).

4. U.S. Dept. of Commerce, Bureau of Public Roads, *Highway Statistics: Summary to 1955* 24 (1957) (tab. MV-201).

continues to do so. Having written the first and still the best-known demystified statement of a judge's philosophy of adjudication, Cardozo was expected to be an outstanding judge. A lawyer could, of course, be a fine scholar and a mediocre judge (some would find this combination exemplified in the career of Felix Frankfurter).[5] But we know that Cardozo was not a mediocre judge—that he was in fact outstanding—and this both lends authority to his statement of his judicial philosophy and enables the statement to reinforce his judicial reputation.

4. Cardozo was an attractive human being. He elicits sympathy and affection, not merely admiration. High achievers tend not to be likable; when they are, we like them all the more and extend some of our favor to the work itself. In addition, Cardozo's personal qualities probably enabled him to get his way in the New York Court of Appeals more often than a less sympathetic personality could have done. (Those qualities may also underlie his ingratiating rhetoric.) Cardozo was rarely in dissent on that court, and all his famous innovative opinions are majority opinions. He must have had a knack for carrying his colleagues with him. I doubt whether he owed this knack entirely to his power of legal reasoning or rhetoric. I think he owed it in significant part to the flattering solicitude with which he treated his colleagues, without going overboard in that direction as Felix Frankfurter was later to do on the Supreme Court. The impact of this solicitude was amplified by the conditions under which the judges of the court of appeals worked. During the term they lived in the same small hotel in Albany and took virtually all their meals together. These close quarters enabled Cardozo to work his charm on his colleagues to maximum effect.

5. I do not share this assessment, but I do think that Frankfurter was not as fine a judge as his pre-judicial career promised. He was widely expected (not least by himself) to be another Holmes or Brandeis. Despite his great intelligence he was not in the league of either Holmes or Brandeis as a judge—mainly for reasons of temperament but partly perhaps from trying too self-consciously to model himself on those illustrious predecessors.

Two anecdotes told by Frankfurter will underscore the point, even after they are discounted for possible exaggeration. Frankfurter said that he had never understood the Catholic doctrine of Adoration until he witnessed Judge Cuthbert Pound's attitude toward Cardozo; and that the other judges of the New York Court of Appeals read books because Cardozo liked to discuss books at the dinner table in Albany.

All this was lost when Cardozo went to Washington and may explain in part his evident unhappiness there. But probably a more important cause was the highly political character of Supreme Court adjudication, which did not suit Cardozo's temperament or experience as it did those of Jackson and Black, for example.

Cardozo's magic on the New York court must not be overstated. My impression from the opinions of his colleagues is that throughout his service on the court most of his colleagues were, like him, political moderates with modestly progressive leanings, although it is interesting to note that, as a Democrat, Cardozo was in the minority on the court.[6] His task, in the performance of which he excelled, was not to persuade his colleagues to change their principles (a task beyond the persuasive power of any judge), but to persuade them to give rein to those principles. He showed them how to write professionally respectable opinions changing the law in the direction they and he desired.

Likability, politeness, and skill in personal relations do not exhaust the personal side of the reputation equation. There is also *character*, in the sense of integrity and trustworthiness. Character is important to a judicial reputation because in dealing with the

6. Francis Bergan, *The History of the New York Court of Appeals, 1847–1932* (1985), lists the political party affiliations of most, though not all, of the judges who served on the New York Court of Appeals with Cardozo. By my count of the number of Democrats and number of Republicans on the court each year in which Cardozo served (excluding 1932, in which he served for only two months before leaving for the Supreme Court)—and ignoring the lone Progressive and the judges who had no party affiliation (or whose affiliation Bergen does not note)—the court was on average 40 percent Democrat, 60 percent Republican.

work of judges we inevitably take much on faith. Appellate decision making in the American legal system is characterized by a high degree of uncertainty. This makes it difficult to assess a judicial decision without access, which often is itself difficult and time-consuming to obtain, to briefs and lower-court records, and without careful study of the precedents and the other sources of law at the time of the decision under examination. In the presence of uncertainty, people grasp at straws. Powerful rhetoric is one of these straws; the business of rhetoric, as Aristotle famously explained, is to persuade on matters of uncertainty. Character is another such straw. This is the insight that underlies the rhetorical device known as the "ethical appeal," that is, the speaker's effort to portray himself as a person whose words can be trusted: a person of character, in other words. Incorruptible, scandal-free, moderate, seemingly apolitical, not given to (visible) self-aggrandizement, Cardozo radiated character. This made it more likely that other judges, academics, and practicing lawyers would give his opinions the benefit of the doubt—thinking that if they were minded to disagree perhaps it was their judgment that was at fault, not Cardozo's.

5. Cardozo cultivated the good opinion of academics. He did this in his program of extrajudicial writings, which are studded with flattering references to the work of legal academics; in his opinions, which cite academic writings far more frequently than was customary among his judicial colleagues (see table 8 below); and in his support of, and work with academics in, the American Law Institute, primarily an academic project. Academics are human; they reciprocated his attention.

Yet I would give all five of these factors together no more weight than either of the first two I mentioned—rhetoric and pragmatism (realism, instrumentalism, antiformalism)—in explaining Cardozo's professional eminence. This weighting underscores the normative ambiguity of "reputation" or "eminence." I have ascribed Cardozo's great reputation to a combination of factors of which some have little or even no positive normative valence. I have put at the head of the list a factor famously equivocal from a normative standpoint—rhetorical skill. And I have said nothing about Cardozo's analytical power. Is all this a prelude to declaring Cardozo's reputation unearned or exaggerated?

It would be if Cardozo had been a law professor rather than a judge. But it is a mistake to suppose that the best judge is the judge who most resembles the best law professor or that the best judicial opinion is the one that most closely resembles an excellent law-review article. Judges do not work under conditions that enable them to produce opinions of high academic quality; so a judge having academic aspirations for his opinions is likely to be a flop. The subject-matter jurisdiction of most major American courts is too broad to enable specialization, especially in a court where opinions are assigned by rotation or other random process; so the judges are bound to know less about each field than the professors in those fields know. Furthermore, the length of time available for preparing an opinion is too short to enable research, discussion, and reflection of academic depth and intensity. And like Cardozo, most judges are appointed from practice, which means they had either explicitly or implicitly rejected an academic career years earlier. In any event, few legal academics have been successful who did not become academics early in their legal careers, and we therefore should not expect lawyers appointed to the bench after many years of practice to write judicial opinions of high academic quality even if they had been frustrated academics all those years. Then too the audience for judicial opinions is not primarily an academic one. Finally, the judge who wants to be effective is constrained for the most part to operate incrementally, respecting distinctions, precedents, traditions, and whatnot that make the professor justifiably impatient.

For all these reasons we should not expect a high order either of intellectual creativity or of analytical rigor in even the best judicial opinions. But what we can expect, and what we find in abundance in Cardozo's opinions, are (1) a vivid, even dramatic, bodying forth of the judge's concerns, (2) a lucid presentation of arresting particulars—fodder for academic analysis, (3) a sense of the relatedness of these particulars to larger themes, (4) a point of view that transcends the litigants' parochial concerns (for Cardozo it was his pragmatist program), (5) a power of clear and forceful statement, and (6) a high degree of sensitivity to the expectations of one's audience. Anyone conversant with literature will recognize these as virtues commonly associated with works of imaginative literature and therefore rhetorical.

Pursuing the literary analogy we may say that a prime virtue of a judicial opinion is wit in the eighteenth-century sense of what oft was thought but ne'er so well expressed. None of the themes in Cardozo's judicial oeuvre is novel, and they are played in cases randomly served from the docket. The skill lies in making each of them a memorable exemplar of an issue, problem, or approach. It is an essentially literary skill, which Cardozo possessed to a high degree. He was also a highly competent legal analyst but no more so than many judges who are deservedly much less eminent than he. I suspect that the disquiet that many academic lawyers feel about Cardozo comes from a reluctance to acknowledge that so "unprofessional" a skill as literary writing ability could make a judge great. The academic—the lawyer generally—may admit that law may sometimes be poetry but is unlikely to admit that poetry may sometimes be law. The tendency of academics is to view judges (implicitly) as failed academics, to be flayed for the amusement of students. Natural as it is, this tendency misconceives the proper division of labor between the judge and the professor. The judge is not to compete with the professor but to engage freshly, fruitfully, vivaciously, constructively, and expeditiously with the disputes that he is called on to resolve.

Table 8 quantifies some stylistic characteristics of Cardozo's opinions. The comparison is between a random sample of sixty Cardozo opinions (all in the New York Court of Appeals) and an equal number of opinions by Cardozo's colleagues, selected as in

TABLE 8
Stylistic Comparison, Cardozo
and Non-Cardozo Opinions

|  | Cardozo | Non-Cardozo |
| --- | --- | --- |
| Average words per sentence | 21.5 | 27.8 |
| Average words per opinion | 1,923.3 | 1,785.0 |
| Number of cases cited | 20.8 | 7.3 |
| Number of scholarly citations | 2.3 | 0.6 |

chapter 5. Cardozo's sentences are shorter, making for a crisper, more dramatic style than that of his colleagues. His opinions are slightly longer but more compact, for they contain three times as many citations as his colleagues' opinions do.[7] He achieves this economy by refusing to follow his colleagues' deadly practice of discussing individual cases at length. He cites almost four times as many scholarly works as his colleagues,[8] illustrating my previous point that Cardozo cultivated academics. Since, despite Cardozo's terseness, his opinions contain on average almost twice as many case citations as his colleagues' opinions do, the impression the opinions convey is very much a professional one. Cardozo is not defying the craft standard that requires judicial opinions to be rich in citations. This richness helped make his innovations and other novelties palatable to the profession, notably in the *MacPherson* case as I remarked in chapter 6.

7. By national as well as by New York standards. The state supreme courts studied by Professor Friedman and his colleagues cited, in the period (1915–1925) that is most comparable to Cardozo's tenure on the New York Court of Appeals, an average of 9.8 cases per opinion. Friedman et al., note 3 above, at 796 (tab. 6). My figure of three times as many is from adding the last two rows in table 8.

8. Similarly, a study of citations by justices of the Supreme Court of California reveals that Justice Traynor cited two and a half times as many secondary authorities as the average of his colleagues. John Henry Merryman, "The Authority of Authority: What the California Supreme Court Cited in 1950," 6 *Stanford Law Review* 613, 656–662 (1954). A later study by Merryman points out that Traynor cited more of all sorts of authority than his colleagues—just like Cardozo. Merryman, note 3 above, at 422.

In stressing the rhetorical side of Cardozo's opinions I may seem to be belittling him. That is not my intention. An industrial analogy may be helpful. One of the persistent Marxist fallacies is the idea that production is more worthwhile socially than distribution, marketing, and other services—that what comes earlier in the chain of production and distribution is somehow better, more important, than what comes later. An equally stubborn fallacy is that analytical power is more basic, and *therefore* more meritorious, than expressive skills. This ordering is related to a deep-seated but simplistic epistemology in which thought precedes speech. The ordering is unwarranted even if the epistemology is accepted. Temporal priority does not dictate merit. Just as production is useless without distribution, so analytical power is useless without the power to communicate the results of its exercise. The enormous output of American courts places a correspondingly enormous premium on expressive skills. And that output is truly enormous. Between 1895 and the end of 1989, the West Publishing Company, which publishes the opinions of the principal American courts, received 2,819,635 opinions for publication.[9] All of them are still in print. All are still accessible for citation or reprinting (judicial opinions are not copyrighted). The power of vivid statement lifts an opinion by a Cardozo, a Holmes, a Learned Hand out of the swarm of humdrum, often numbing, judicial opinions, rivets attention, crystallizes relevant concerns and considerations, provokes thought. These are services of great value to the profession. And, odd as it may seem, they are linked to the program of a pragmatic jurisprudence. Pragmatism is not only, or even mainly, policy analysis. It is also and more fundamentally the rejection of a sharp line between truth and rhetoric, between the analytic and the persuasive, the discursive and the metaphoric; it is recognition that knowledge advances through changes in perspective as well as

9. Letter to the author from John C. Smith, Editorial Counsel, West Publishing Company, February 7, 1990.

through patient accretions.[10] The judicial opinion that provokes thought by the force of its rhetoric may also advance thought.

I have been discussing good judicial rhetoric, or the good in judicial rhetoric. There is also a bad judicial rhetoric, which consists of such familiar but unedifying lawyers' tactics as distorting the facts, and it is a rhetoric to which Cardozo at times descended, most strikingly in the *Palsgraf* case; the suppression of the reason for the plaintiff's suing the parent rather than the subsidiary corporation in *Berkey* is also disturbing. A balanced assessment of Cardozo's performance as a judge must weight his considerable rhetorical power, his worthy pragmatic program, and his general soundness against his rhetorical sins both of commission and of omission and his frequent failure to follow through on the pragmatic program by candidly displaying and analyzing the practical considerations bearing on decision. No doubt the rhetorical sins reflect Cardozo's nearly twenty-three years as a litigator. So deep an immersion in adversarial practice could not fail to leave an indelible stamp in light of which his judicial opinions were bound on occasion to exhibit the characteristic excesses of a lawyer's brief. Cardozo's experience at the bar was a source of strength to him; it gave him credibility with lawyers and his fellow judges, and it showed him how to write opinions that bench and bar would accept. But every strength has its weakness; and the weakness of this particular strength was the occasional lapse into the adversarial mode.

I do not want to exaggerate. My study of the briefs and records persuades me that the handling of facts in Cardozo's opinions is for the most part accurate, although not scrupulously fair—at least, not generous—to the losing party. Still, it is evident that not only was Cardozo not a saint; he was not a perfect judge. But if there are trade-offs between rhetorical power and factual accuracy, and if a long career as a litigating lawyer both helps and hinders judicial performance, perfection in adjudication may be

10. I emphasize this in *The Problems of Jurisprudence* (1990), esp. ch. 4.

unattainable. So what else is new? For, these subtleties to one side, it is apparent that there are no perfect judges, just as there are no perfect hitters in baseball. The conditions of employment and the nature of the judicial game conspire to prevent perfection. Only by comparing Cardozo to other notable judges can we fix his rank.

The citations evidence—analogous to baseball statistics—presented in chapter 5 is relevant to this comparison. But, illustrating one of the limitations of citation studies, exact comparison among judges is feasible only with respect to judges serving at the same time on the same court. We can say with confidence that Cardozo was a greater judge than Frederick Crane or Cuthbert Pound or anyone else with whom Cardozo served for a substantial period of time on the New York Court of Appeals, but if we want to compare Cardozo with judges as famous as he, such as Holmes, Brandeis, and Learned Hand, we are confined to speculation. So let us speculate. The comparison with Holmes is particularly intriguing. Like Cardozo, he had long service on a state court, culminating in his appointment as chief judge, before elevation to the Supreme Court. Also like Cardozo he was the author of celebrated extrajudicial writings, a specialist in the common law, a pragmatist and antiformalist (though less consistently so than Cardozo), and a notable rhetorician. Although they were men of different generations, Holmes having been born in 1841 and Cardozo in 1870, their careers as appellate judges overlapped by eighteen years—from 1914, when Cardozo was appointed to the New York Court of Appeals, to 1932, when Holmes resigned from the Supreme Court.

Holmes is, of course, the larger figure, as the early tables in chapter 5 suggest. He was a judge for twice as long as Cardozo, and his service on the Supreme Court was five times the length of Cardozo's. He had the more penetrating, seminal intellect; his extrajudicial writings are more original and important than Cardozo's by a wide margin. And he was the most eloquent judge who ever wrote; perhaps his only peers as American masters of prose are Abraham Lincoln and Henry James. Holmes in his extrajudicial writings placed as strong an individual stamp on tort and contract law as Cardozo was to do in his judicial opinions, and as a Supreme Court justice he shaped the law of free speech, economic due process, and habeas corpus and became the preeminent spokesman for judicial self-restraint. In breadth and depth his achievement exceeds Cardozo's, as it does that of any other judge since John Marshall, and perhaps of any other judge, period. Yet had Holmes died after six years on the Supreme Court he would be considered today a lesser judge than Cardozo, though a greater legal figure overall. A less conscientious—indeed, less *ambitious*—judge (although a more ambitious person) than Cardozo, and also, and relatedly, less interested in playing games with precedent and hence Cardozo's superior in candor, Holmes made little attempt as a justice of the Massachusetts Supreme Judicial Court to seize the opportunities that lay at hand to shape the common law fields in which he was so expert.[11] A curious passivity seems to have descended on Holmes the state judge until toward the end of his stay the Massachusetts court encountered a rising tide of public law cases that fascinated Holmes and paved the way for the accomplishments of his Supreme Court years.[12] His judicial performance exhibits greater variance than Cardozo's. Cardozo was steadier, but his average performance was below Holmes's. Holmes was a genius, but his opinions contain a much higher proportion of analytical flaws and unreasoned assertions than Cardozo's do.[13] Although Cardozo revered Holmes, he was by no means a slavish follower, and in particular took a more flexible view of contract—an area in which

11. Mark Tushnet, "The Logic of Experience: Oliver Wendell Holmes on the Supreme Judicial Court," 63 *Virginia Law Review* 975 (1977).

12. These opinions, many collected in *The Judicial Opinions of Oliver Wendell Holmes: Constitutional Opinions, Selected Excerpts and Epigrams as Given in the Supreme Judicial Court of Massachusetts* (1883–1902) (Harry C. Shriver ed. 1940), deserve more attention than they have received. Many of them are gems.

13. Tushnet, note 11 above, esp. p. 1017; Richard A. Posner, *Law and Literature: A Misunderstood Relation* 281–289 (1988), and references cited there.

Holmes displayed, albeit intermittently, a penchant for formalism—than Holmes did. Neither judge was as scrupulous about factual accuracy as—I believe—he should have been, although I recognize the tension between the literary and the accurate. Finally, reference to Holmes's formalism should help remind us that he had greater intellectual *range* than Cardozo. Cardozo, moderate that he was, steered by the lights of a moderate pragmatism, while Holmes veered among utilitarianism, other forms of instrumentalism, Social Darwinism, legal formalism, behaviorism, and skepticism.

Cardozo is often bracketed with Brandeis, but this is mainly because both were Jews, both were liberals, and they were roughly contemporary, Brandeis having been born in 1856. As judges they were as different as could be unless you think a judge's political slant is the most interesting thing about him. Brandeis had strong political and economic views, many of which seem in retrospect quaint, and which he relentlessly pressed in his opinions on issues of public law.[14] After his early article with Warren on privacy, Brandeis displayed no interest in the common law even though the Supreme Court retained a substantial common law jurisdiction until the (Brandeis) decision in *Erie R.R. v. Tompkins* in 1938. Brandeis wrote with great vigor but for the most part (except in his great *Whitney* and *Olmsted* dissents)[15] without eloquence.

Cardozo's only peers in judicial eloquence, besides Holmes, were Robert Jackson and Learned Hand. Jackson, like Holmes, cultivated a plain style with great success; on occasion—such as the flag-salute case (*Barnette*) and the concurring opinion in

14. Good examples are his dissenting opinion—from which Cardozo politely but carefully dissociated himself—extolling the virtues of a chain-store tax, in Liggett Co. v. Lee, 288 U.S. 517, 541–580 (1933) (Brandeis, J., dissenting); see id. at 580–586 (Cardozo, J., dissenting) and his dissenting opinion in New State Ice Co. v. Liebmann, 285 U.S. 262, 280 (1932), which I discuss in *Economic Analysis of Law* 590–592 (3d ed. 1986).

15. Whitney v. California, 274 U.S. 357, 372–380 (1927); Olmsted v. United States, 277 U.S. 438, 471–485 (1928).

*Dennis*[16]—he soared above Cardozo in eloquence.[17] A far more wordly figure than Cardozo, he came to the Supreme Court from a series of high positions in the Roosevelt administration and was seriously talked of as a possible chief justice—even a possible presidential candidate. His experience in the upper echelons of government lend a resonance to his public-law opinions that has no counterpart in Cardozo's oeuvre. He may have been a better choice for the Supreme Court than Cardozo,[18] but if one may judge (perhaps unfairly) from his weird brief for the estate in the *Allegheny College* case[19] he would have been a questionable choice for a predominantly common law court and might have found service on such a court one long snore.

Learned Hand's half-century as a federal judge in New York overlapped Cardozo's judicial career at both ends. Like Cardozo, Hand placed his stamp on several fields—patents, copyright,

---

16. West Virginia State Board of Education v. Barnette, 319 U.S. 624 (1943); Dennis v. United States, 341 U.S. 494, 561–579 (1951).

17. "He had a 'big' virtuoso style, magnificent and athletic in exposition, powerful and ingenious in argument, racy, sardonic, alive with the passion and wit of his personality. Though grand, it was not grandiloquent. It had the startling changes in pace, the sudden pungencies, the wry ironies that characterize the 'modern' manner." Louis L. Jaffe, "Mr. Justice Jackson," 68 *Harvard Law Review* 940 (1955).

18. Which is not to gainsay Jackson's serious deficiencies in judicial temperament. See Dennis J. Hutchinson, "The Black-Jackson Feud," 1988 *Supreme Court Review* 203.

19. Excerpted and discussed in Alfred S. Konefsky, "How to Read, or at Least Not Misread, Cardozo in the *Allegheny College* Case," 36 *Buffalo Law Review* 645, 697–699 (1987) (App. II). The complete brief sustains the impression created by Konefsky's excerpts. Here is a representative passage: "The law of New York condemns all mental flip flops by Courts in the aid of charity. It is clear though inelastic; honest though rigid. Counsel is, of course, able to cite foreign cases to sustain his argument. In fact, we have found some stronger for him than those he cites. On no subject do we find greater confusion and lack of integrity among our sister states" (p. 15). I imagine that this intemperate argument, so uncharacteristic of the briefs in the New York Court of Appeals, rubbed Cardozo's fur the wrong way. It was especially maladroit in response to the powerful brief filed by Pickard & Pickard on behalf of Allegheny College. Jackson's name is only the third on the brief for the estate, but the style throughout seems to be his.

trademarks, and unfair competition most directly, but also free speech, statutory interpretation, antitrust, and, most pertinently, tort law: his opinions in *Carroll Towing* and *T.J. Hooper* are landmarks of tort law. Like Cardozo, Hand was an eloquent judge, but their writing styles differ interestingly. Cardozo's has a high sheen, an artifactual quality; we are conscious of his opinions as works of judicial art. Hand's opinions are successful imitations of the judge's thinking process as he wrestles with a case. It twists and turns as the judge is pulled now hither, now yon, by the weight of opposing considerations as they present themselves to his mind. Hand is the Henry James of judicial stylists. Cardozo's style suggests a smoother surface, Hand's a greater depth. There is a parallel in their personalities. With his famous rudeness to lawyers at oral argument and his notorious table manners, Hand was as rough as Cardozo was smooth; yet they were good, although not close, friends. Hand's cases were more difficult than Cardozo's; intuitions of simple justice provided less guidance; and his opinions reveal a broader and more powerful intellect than Cardozo, a better feel for policy, a greater candor and scrupulousness, but less verve and dash. Although they were contemporaries, Hand seems the more modern of the two; yet this may be in large part because federal law so fills the current horizon and because he wrote opinions for two decades after Cardozo died. A further complication in comparing the two is that Hand wrote several times as many opinions as Cardozo. This was not because he was the more productive judge—not necessarily, anyway. Not only was Hand a judge for twice as long as Cardozo but judges who sit in panels of three, as federal court of appeals judges do (except for the rare *en banc*), write more opinions per year than judges who sit in larger panels; there are fewer judges to share the opinion-writing burden.

All the judges I have mentioned are *stronger* judicial personalities than Cardozo: more opinionated, more aggressive intellectually, more programmatic. Of all the great judges of his (approximate) time Cardozo is perhaps the most neutral, the most even, the most at home in the legal profession, the most a comfortable insider: the most *professional* judge. This may be why, in the long run, he was perhaps the least influential of the great judges in changing the direction of the law.

Yet among state court judges of this century Cardozo has no peer, and perhaps we should leave it at that, while recognizing that with the displacement of more and more formerly state law cases into the federal courts because of the relentless expansion of federal law it is becoming increasingly difficult for a state judge to make a mark. It would be silly to try to rank Cardozo among the all-time great American judges, but I am convinced that, despite his failings, which I have stressed perhaps more than his admirers would wish, he deserves to be called a great judge. I predict that anyone who will take the time to read the briefs and lower-court opinions in Cardozo's best-known cases will reach the same conclusion.

Yet is it not a source of abiding disquiet that not only Cardozo but most of the other "great" judges have been master rhetoricians? Even if rhetoric is a vital dimension of judicial performance at the appellate level (the only level I am considering), is there not room for the brilliant analyst who is not a skillful or self-conscious writer? Surely there is, but to pursue this question is to underscore once more the normatively equivocal character of "reputation." Reputation is, we recall, bestowed on the "reputee," not created by him. The competent, even brilliant, analysis of yesterday's legal problems has little current interest, in part because a major task of reconstruction may be necessary to determine that it was brilliant. The sparkling, vivid, memorable opinion is not so chained to the immediate context of its creation. It can be pulled out and made exemplary of law's durable concerns. That is, it is literature; literature is the body of texts that survive the context in which they were created because they speak to us today.[20] The literary judge wears best over time.

20. John M. Ellis, *The Theory of Literary Criticism: A Logical Analysis* (1974); Posner, note 13 above, esp. ch. 2.

# *Epilogue*

## Vistas in Research

THE PRESENT STUDY, though limited to a single judge, invites consideration of several avenues of further research. I sketch ten of these—very briefly—in this epilogue.

1. I have sampled Cardozo's opinions, leaving many undiscussed. My studies of citations to his opinions and to those of his colleagues on the New York Court of Appeals were also based on samples of his opinions rather than on the entire corpus. The hypotheses proposed in this paper concerning Cardozo's achievement should be tested on the unstudied portion of his work.

2. I have examined the briefs in only twenty of Cardozo's cases and in none of the cases assigned to his colleagues. The modest size of the sample and the lack of comparison make it difficult to assess the "value added" of Cardozo's opinions with precision and confidence, and yet I have little doubt that he did not stick as closely to the briefs as his colleagues did. Despite much pretense to the contrary by judges and lawyers, it is one of the marks of the great judge to recast the issues in cases in his own image rather than to assume a passive, "umpireal" stance. We need more studies that compare judges' opinions with the lawyers' briefs in their cases.

I said that the briefs in Cardozo's cases appear to be superior to modern briefs, just as Cardozo's opinions are superior to modern opinions. Could it be that the character of appellate adjudication has changed since his time, from a handicraft system characterized by high average quality of product to a mass-production system not necessarily inferior overall but characterized by lower average quality? This is another rich area for further study.

3. Before I began this study I thought that the common practice in state supreme courts of assigning opinions by rotation or random draw[1] was awful, because it failed to sort opinions to judges according to the judges' individual interests and abilities. Seeing how Cardozo and his court thrived under such a system, I have begun to rethink my prejudice.

(a) The rotation system retards subject-matter specialization, but as specialization on a court of general and broad jurisdiction has inherent limitations, perhaps there is little or even no net loss. Moreover, on a court of generalists there is a danger that a judge who happens to have specialized knowledge of a particular field will overawe his colleagues in that field, perhaps making a court of seven or nine or however many judges effectively a court of one. Rotation reduces that danger.

(b) Rotation weakens the power of the chief judge—which may be all to the good. A system in which judges toady to the chief in order to obtain the prize assignments is not necessarily a healthy system. The rotation system encourages each judge to do the very best he can with each case, knowing that he will not be able to blame the shortcomings in his performance on the enmity of his chief or bask in the chief's favor.

(c) A related point is that rotation facilitates comparison between judges. It makes clear to them that a judicial career is what the judge makes of it.

(d) Rotation reduces rivalry and resentment among judges and by doing so promotes collegiality and cooperation. Since competition is a goad to excellence, there is loss as well as gain. How-

---

1. In Cardozo's day, at any rate, the opinion was assigned before argument, and the judge to whom it was assigned was required to write a brief memo for circulation to his colleagues before the oral argument. (A practice, incidentally, that may well give the randomly assigned judge an undue influence on the vote.) The New York Court of Appeals steadfastly refuses to make Cardozo's, or any other judge's, pre-argument memos available to scholars.

ever, the rotation system promotes a form of competition—what in public utility regulation is called "yardstick competition." In a system of assignment by rotation, each judge is drawing his cards from a randomly shuffled pack. By studying how each judge plays the hand dealt him, we can form a judgment of his ability that is not blurred by considerations of his success in extracting favorable treatment from the chief judge—and maybe he is the chief judge, and favors himself.[2]

A brief discussion of assignment by rotation by Cardozo's predecessor as chief judge of the New York Court of Appeals makes several of my points and is worth quotation in full:

> As is generally known, cases are taken by judges in that Court [the New York Court of Appeals] by rotation, and after a long experience I feel very strongly that this is a better method than that of assignment of cases by the Chief Judge, such as is practiced in many other courts including the Supreme Court of the United States. No one need think that a judge of an appellate court does not continue to be human enough to appreciate the difference between a case with a voluminous record, complicated facts and questions of no particular or general interest and a case on the other hand which does involve interesting questions of general importance. While he does his duty and takes whatever comes to him he finds one case interesting and an intellectual pleasure and the other one a piece of drudgery. It is difficult to imagine a Chief Judge endowed with such tact and wisdom that in the assignment of cases he would not occasionally make some associate judge feel disappointed that he received some unattractive case and did not receive some more interesting one. In addition it seems to me that the process of assignment might easily result in the development of specialists which is the last thing that is desirable in an appellate court where a case ought to receive the independent consideration and judgment of every member. For instance, it would seem that if a case came before the Court invoking questions of irrigation, patent rights, taxation or land titles, it would be quite natural for a Chief Judge to send it to some member of the

2. Notice that, to defeat strategizing, it is essential that a rotation system provide for assignment of replacement cases by a random method. That is, a judge must not know what case he will be assigned in the event that he takes a position on an assigned case that fails to command a majority, resulting in the reassignment of that case to another judge and the assignment of another case to him in its place.

Court who had special experience in cases dealing with those particular questions, and that it would be equally natural for other judges, unconsciously, to think they might safely rely on the judgment of one who had become a specialist in that class of cases and thus fail to exercise that independent judgment which litigants are entitled to expect from every member of an appellate court.[3]

I do not want to offer a final judgment on assignment by rotation. As pointed out in the rather limited scholarly literature on systems of opinion assignment,[4] rotation has the major disadvantage of preventing assignment to the judge who—all questions of specialized knowledge to one side—may be best able to write an opinion that will command a majority.[5] All I suggest is that it is high time we had a systematic study of the different methods of assigning opinions.

4. Reference to what might be termed the communitarian aspects of assignment by rotation leads naturally to a more fundamental question: should majority opinions be signed, or should not all majority opinions be per curiam opinions? The practice of the signed opinion exerts a centrifugal influence on the work of a court. It identifies the opinion as an individual work, which encourages the authoring judge to individualize it and the other judges to accept its idiosyncrasies out of respect for individual difference and personality and out of desire for reciprocal treatment ("live and let live"). The temptation is to make a judicial opinion an exercise in self-advertisement and self-aggrandisement, and is enhanced by the eminence that has accrued to judges (such as

3. Frank H. Hiscock, "The Court of Appeals of New York: Some Features of Its Organization and Work," 14 *Cornell Law Quarterly* 131, 138 (1929).

4. Melinda Gann Hall, "Opinion Assignment Procedures and Conference Practices in State Supreme Courts," 73 *Judicature* 209 (1990), and references cited therein. Hall notes that 70 percent of state supreme courts use a rotation or other random system. *Id.* at 210 (tab. 1). See also Elliot E. Slotnick, "Who Speaks for the Court? The View from the States," 26 *Emory Law Journal* 107 (1977).

5. On the strategic use of the assignment power in the Supreme Court, see Elliot E. Slotnick, "Who Speaks for the Court? Majority Opinion Assignment from Taft to Burger," 23 *American Journal of Political Science* 60 (1979).

Cardozo) who write highly individualistic opinions. In addition, the institution of the signed opinion enables a judge to cultivate an admiring audience outside of, and even antagonistic to, his judicial colleagues, and this reaching outside of the court for praise can engender tensions within the court. It can also, however, encourage judicial independence.

The other side of the coin is that anonymity diffuses responsibility and by doing so diminishes a sense of responsibility. (It might by the same token encourage judicial independence; independence and irresponsibility are not entirely unrelated.) The author of a per curiam opinion may be less diligent and conscientious than the author of a signed opinion, knowing that the public will accord him only one-ninth of the blame (in a court of nine judges) for his mistakes and only one-ninth of the praise for his insights and aphorisms. The anonymity of appellate judging in a system without signed majority opinions would reduce the attractions of a judicial career to some of the ablest lawyers; but whether the average quality of appellate decision making would fall is uncertain. Continental European judiciaries, it should be noted, do not issue signed majority opinions. The practice seems to work well enough for them—but how it would work for us is difficult to say. Perhaps it would work better today, when most judicial opinions are written by the judges' law clerks rather than by the judges themselves, than it would have before opinion writing was delegated. Or perhaps it would just lead to a flood of concurring opinions, as judges strove to reestablish their individuality.

Here in any event is a rich subject for study, and one close to the heart of this book: without signed opinions, very few appellate judges would *have* a reputation to study.

5. If I am correct that judicial eminence is—and rightly so—a function in major part of judicial eloquence, we need more studies of the literary dimension of opinion writing,[6] and we

6. And studies that link the analysis of judicial rhetoric to the analysis of po-

need to begin thinking about whether the decline in humanities education, which both reflects and is reflected in the decline of the ability of Americans, including judges, to write lucid and elegant prose, requires changes in the way in which we organize our legal system. More broadly, we need to pay attention to precisely what it is that we value in appellate judges. It is easy to list desiderata, but we must go beyond platitudes, identify trade-offs, and describe the *attainable* judicial ideal. This means that we need more studies of judges, including judges who are not famous. How much better really was Cardozo than his colleagues? Citation studies are suggestive, not conclusive.

6. The present study opens up the heretofore neglected field of quantitative analysis of judicial reputation, influence, and achievement. The legal profession, even on the academic side, resists quantitative analysis—and sometimes defends its resistance by invoking the humanistic values whose passing I have just lamented. Quantitative does not equal philistine, and television is a greater threat to eloquence than statistics is. I hope this study will encourage further efforts to bring measurement to bear on issues central to the legal process.

7. More, surely, can be done with the vexing question of judicial *influence* than I have done. But it will have to be done by scholars steeped in the history of the particular fields in which particular judges worked. To determine the true impact of *Mac-Pherson,* for example—to go beyond an impressionistic sense that it changed the law—would require close study not only of the New York precedents but also of developments in the law of other states that may have presaged a parallel evolution to that of New

litical rhetoric generally, an analysis illustrated by James T. Boulton, *The Language of Politics in the Age of Wilkes and Burke* (1963), esp. chs. 7 and 8 (dealing with Burke's *Reflections on the Revolution in France* and Paine's *Rights of Man*); Robert T. Oliver, *The Influence of Rhetoric in the Shaping of Great Britain: From the Roman Invasion to the Early Nineteenth Century* (1986); Lionel Crocker, *An Analysis of Lincoln and Douglas as Public Speakers and Debaters* (1968), esp. pt. 3; Halford Ross Ryan, "Roosevelt's First Inaugural: A Study of Technique," 65 *Quarterly Journal of Speech* 137 (1979).

York law, even if there had never been a *MacPherson* case. The question how much difference "great" judges make ties in with the question of signed versus per curiam opinions. The signed opinion may invite greatness, but perhaps the great judge is more an ornament than an engine of legal progress.

8. Reputation is a pervasive and important feature of social life. Remarkably little systematic work has been done on it. Here, too, I hope this study will light a beacon for scholars.

9. The Mead LEXIS law-review data base (chapter 5) provides a rich mine for studies of legal scholarship, judicial reputation, and reputation generally. (So does the *Social Sciences Citation Index,* which includes a large number of law reviews in its data base.) I have done very little with it in this study. I have not, for example, corrected for the number of mentions of a judge or scholar within articles, as distinct from the number of articles that mention him. And I have not tried to differentiate between articles and student notes, or between leading and lesser law reviews. Judicial and other legal reputations may be stratified in interesting ways that these and other refinements of my analysis might reveal.

10. I hope that this book will encourage further ventures in the new genre that I have dubbed the critical judicial study. For better or for worse, the legal system has its superstars, and most of them—or at least the most luminous of them—are judges. (At least this has been so historically; it may well be changing.) Since few judges, even among the most illustrious, lead interesting lives, the scope for judicial biography is limited. The scholarly promise of critical studies of individual judges' work may not be.

# Index